Xtreme
Faith

Rick Thomas

DEDICATION

This book is dedicated to Dr. John Avanzini. He has been a spiritual mentor whose valuable insights have greatly strengthened my ministry. His books have been an inspiration to me and have provided a foundation for many of the principles I am sharing in these pages.

Contents

INTRODUCTION

What you are about to read is not written to simply motivate or encourage you. This is not a book that tells you how to acquire just enough hope, belief or expectation to be an average, comfortable Christian.

Instead, get ready to be challenged to take the faith God has placed within you and see it multiplied beyond anything you have ever experienced. Instead of mediocre faith, you are about to come face to face with Xtreme Faith—and learn how it can be yours!

The reason I believe God for the impossible is that I have personally seen the Almighty at work in my own family and ministry. Chapter one is the account of how our faith was tested when my wife, Kathy, faced a life-threatening attack of cancer.

In these pages you will discover:

- How the Lord transforms the invisible into reality
- The secret of tapping into God's unlimited supply

- How your words can enlarge and extend your faith
- Steps that lead from doubting to doing
- How to break the cycle of insufficiency
- Why God requires an internal house-cleaning
- The ingredients of ever-expanding faith – and much more

I want to share the *reasons* God honored the Xtreme faith of Noah, Abraham, Jacob and Moses—and how you can apply the same divine principles today.

Most importantly, you will learn how to enter into a covenant with the Almighty that will produce miracle results.

I pray this book will lift you from your comfort zone and you will experience heaven-sent, life-changing Xtreme Faith.

—Rick Thomas

CHAPTER ONE

"I AM GOING TO LIVE!"

It was June, 2004. My wife, Kathy, and I had just experienced one of the most memorable events in our lives. With our family by our side, we joyfully celebrated our 25th wedding anniversary, complete with a wonderful renewal ceremony our entire congregation witnessed.

Two weeks prior to our anniversary, Kathy discovered a lump in her breast, which she brushed aside because she was so busy with our upcoming hectic schedule.

About three days after the celebration, as we were preparing to leave on a long-planned second honeymoon to Europe, Kathy turned to me and said, "Honey, I believe the lump has grown and I really feel I need to see a doctor before we leave."

We quickly made an appointment to have an ultrasound sonogram taken—not just a mammogram. Kathy told the medical professional, "I need the results immediately. Don't just send them to the surgeon. We're leaving on a trip and I need to know for my peace of mind."

All he would tell her was, "Yes, I do see what may be a mass, but you will really have to consult with your physician."

"I Don't Like What I See"

After praying over and discussing the situation, we decided to go ahead with our trip to Europe and take care of the matter when we returned—of course, all that had just transpired was impossible to erase from our minds.

Immediately after returning to South Florida, Kathy received a call from the surgeon asking her to come in for a consultation.

At the session, the doctor said, "I don't like what I see. We need to do a biopsy."

The appointment was set, but before my wife returned, she also felt a lump in the other side—and under her arm, around the lymph nodes.

During the biopsy, Kathy told the surgeon, "Look

at this. It seems it is expanding and growing rapidly."

"I see that," the surgeon responded, "We'd better do two or three procedures today."

Kathy knew it was serious when the doctor sent for the pathologist and told him, "I need an answer back within the hour."

"WHERE IS YOUR HUSBAND?"

In less than 60 minutes the results arrived, and after pouring over the lab data for a few minutes, the surgeon turned to Kathy and said, "It looks like you have breast cancer."

Those words flew right over Kathy's head and she instinctively responded, "I don't think so."

The surgeon continued, "I'm not sure you fully understand what I am trying to tell you. Where is your husband?"

"He's just outside in the waiting room," Kathy answered.

When I walked into the office, the doctor looked at both of us and uttered five words no one wants to hear: "Your wife has breast cancer."

IN THE FAMILY

With tears welling up in her eyes and pain in her body, Kathy looked at the surgeon. But her faith stretched far beyond her pain.

You see, in our ministry, my wife has taught faith and written songs and sung on the topic. She knows what mighty miracles God can perform, so she confidently said to the physician, "I am going to live and not die!"

This was a powerful statement—especially since her family had a history of cancer. Genetics certainly seemed to play a role: Kathy's grandmother died of breast cancer before her fortieth birthday. Her mother had a lumpectomy. Her mother's younger sister died of breast cancer and her baby sister also had a lumpectomy, faced chemotherapy and was a breast cancer survivor.

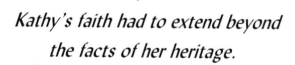

Kathy's faith had to extend beyond the facts of her heritage.

She was being called on to practice what she had been teaching and preaching through the years—not to focus on or fear what was visible, rather to look at what was unseen (2 Corinthians 4:18). She was called upon to employ Xtreme Faith.

"I COULDN'T SLEEP"

Faith doesn't mean you act foolishly and ignore the advice of doctors. Kathy underwent breast cancer surgery and started on chemotherapy treatments.

I believe physicians and surgeons are specially gifted of God to help us—but at the same time they cannot heal you.

Through this physical ordeal, we stayed in the Word of God and continued in ministry. Even though she was on chemo, Kathy still led praise and worship in the church services—and the Lord blessed her by giving her a song.

In Kathy's own words, here is what happened:

The morning after I came home from surgery, I couldn't sleep because I had to lie in one position; I couldn't flip over. My back was aching so I thought I'd go downstairs and sit in an easy chair. But God spoke and told me, "Get up and find your Bible."

"What does He want me to read?"—I wondered. I opened the Old Testament, turned to 2 Samuel 22 and began to read how David

had to literally praise his way through the circumstances he was facing. He talked about his great God in the words of song.

It was seven o'clock in the morning and I was reading who my God was: "The Lord is my rock, my fortress and my deliverer...my shield and the horn of my salvation. He is my stronghold, my refuge and my savior" (2 Samuel 22:2-3).

As I began to study the verses, suddenly a song rose up inside me. I immediately started to write the words and melody God gave me—and in my mind I heard all the parts.

The Lord told me, "This is music I want you to teach your choir, so they will sing it back to you during the next several months as you stand there in faith."

Over the next sixteen weeks, I had eight chemotherapy treatments.

I can't begin to describe what it was like to stand on the platform and lead the choir in this God-inspired song. It lifted me into the heavenlies as they sang of the greatness of our Lord to heal and deliver.

Some of the treatments caused me to be extremely sick, but I determined that, with God's help, I was not going to step down from our music ministry. I promised, "Lord, I am going to praise my way through this!"

Now was the time to live what I believed.

During these days, God began to inspire me with other songs with faith-building words such as, "In His presence there is healing, in His presence there is joy."

―――――X―――――

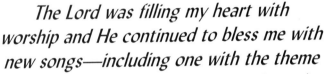

The Lord was filling my heart with worship and He continued to bless me with new songs—including one with the theme of how just one touch from the Master's hand can change everything.

We began to lift our voices in unison and sing these as a congregation, because the words were not just for me, but for others in the body of Christ who were suffering infirmities.

WALKING BY FAITH

While Kathy was going through this process, there

were scores of people who testified to remarkable healings in our church—including cancer.

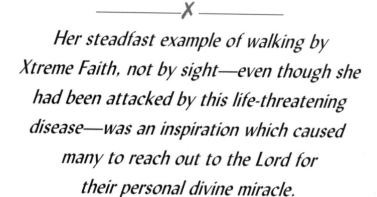

Her steadfast example of walking by Xtreme Faith, not by sight—even though she had been attacked by this life-threatening disease—was an inspiration which caused many to reach out to the Lord for their personal divine miracle.

The last four chemo treatments were excruciating because the side-effects attacked Kathy's feet, hands and even her fingertips. You can imagine how difficult it was for her to play the piano while in such pain—yet she did.

It reached the point where she was unable to even put on her shoes.

During the treatments, she continued to share her faith with the Jewish doctor who administered the chemo. "I know who my God is and He is going to heal me through this entire ordeal."

One year later, Kathy returned for her mammogram and was told, "I don't see any problems." Then she

16

heard the words not normally spoken by doctors, "You are cancer free."

Through her entire challenge, Kathy never doubted what the end result was going to be. *"Even though I walk through the valley of the shadow of death, I will fear no evil, for you are with me; your rod and your staff* [Your Word and Your Spirit] *they comfort me"* (Psalm 23:4).

As we will discover in the chapters to follow, with Xtreme Faith in Almighty God, all things are possible.

CHAPTER TWO

THE POWER OF EXPECTATION

In recent years, the Lord has opened wondrous doors of ministry in many parts of the world—and especially in South America. What impresses me about the people in these lands is their pure, believing faith.

There is no "God *may* work wonders," or "The Almighty *might* hear my prayer." It is always, "The Lord *will* answer when I call on Him."

THEY DIDN'T RECOGNIZE JESUS

I am firmly convinced that if we take God at His Word, our uncertainties will be transformed into belief.

Just after the resurrection, two of the disciples were walking on the road to Emmaus, about seven miles from Jerusalem. They were discussing the death of Jesus and rumors of His resurrection. As they became immersed in conversation, the Lord Himself appeared and began walking with them—but they did not recognize Him.

At the time, their faith was so weak, they could hardly believe the reports circulating that He had come out of the grave.

These were the same chosen disciples who had seen Jesus raise people from the dead and feed the 5,000. However, at this moment, their faith could not extend beyond the crucifixion and burial of their beloved Lord.

It seemed the three years of working together in ministry was not enough to sustain them. How could these men evangelize the world if they did not believe Christ had risen from the tomb?

My friend, Jesus had not failed—and neither had the disciples. It was their deficient faith which let them down.

"How Foolish"

As they journeyed together, Jesus spoke concerning the weakness of their faith. He said, *"How foolish you are, and how slow of heart to believe all that the prophets have spoken!"* (Luke 24:25).

Then He reminded them of what the prophets had said concerning Him. But still, their faith was not revived.

When the disciples reached the place where they were

staying, they invited this Man to spend the evening—still not knowing who He was.

However, *"When he was at the table with them, he took bread, gave thanks, broke it and began to give it to them. Then their eyes were opened and they recognized him"* (vv.30-31).

————— *X* —————

I believe that as He reached out to give them the bread, they could see the nail scars in His hands.

Then suddenly, Jesus vanished (v.31).

He could now leave them because their failing faith had been recharged. The disciples said to each other, *"Were not our hearts burning within us while he talked with us on the road and opened the Scriptures to us?"* (v.32).

That same hour they returned to Jerusalem, found other disciples and told them how Jesus had indeed appeared to them. Once more, the Lord stood before the assembled group, showing Himself and saying, *"Peace be with you"* (v.36).

Several of them were frightened, thinking they had seen a ghost. But Jesus asked, *"Why are you troubled,*

21

and why do doubts rise in your minds? Look at my hands and my feet. It is I myself! Touch me and see; a ghost does not have flesh and bones, as you see I have" (vv.38-39).

THE EVIDENCE

One disciple, Thomas, still harbored doubts. His faith had become so weak that he could not even believe the reports of his most trusted friends—those who had seen Jesus alive with their own eyes.

The disciples had a personal encounter with the resurrected Christ, but Thomas said to them, *"Unless I see the nail marks in his hands and put my finger where the nails were, and put my hand into his side, I will not believe it"* (John 20:24).

A few days later, Thomas was with the disciples when suddenly Jesus appeared in the house where they were gathered—even though the doors were locked. Immediately, the Lord turned to Thomas and said, *"Put your finger here; see my hands. Reach out your hand and put it into my side. Stop doubting and believe"* (v.27).

Astonished, Thomas exclaimed, "My Lord and my God!"

Then Jesus told him, *"Because you have seen me, you have believed; blessed are those who have not seen and yet have believed"* (v.29).

The faltering faith of Thomas was transformed by this physical evidence—and Scripture documents that Jesus is alive today!

"INCREASE OUR FAITH"

Don't be reluctant to admit the fact that there are times when your faith is feeble. Those who walked with Jesus when He was on earth certainly weren't shy regarding this matter. *"The apostles said to the Lord, 'Increase our faith!'"* (Luke 17:5).

Here's the exciting news! You can enjoy the same level of faith the apostles possessed. Peter addressed his epistle, *"To those who through the righteousness of our God and Savior Jesus Christ have received a faith as precious as ours"* (2 Peter 1:1).

Be honest concerning your measure of belief and expectation. God knows your heart and will respond to whatever amount of faith you have, but xtreme circumstances call for Xtreme Faith.

EVERYTHING IS POSSIBLE

This is illustrated in the account of the father whose child had a demon. With tears in his eyes, the man came to Jesus and pleaded, *"Teacher, I brought you my son,* who is possessed by a spirit that has robbed him of speech. Whenever it seizes him, it throws him to the ground. He foams at the mouth, gnashes his teeth and becomes rigid" (Mark 9:17-18).

Scripture records that when the spirit saw Jesus, "...it immediately threw the boy into a convulsion. He fell to the ground and rolled around, foaming at the mouth" (v.20).

"How long has he been like this?" asked Jesus.

"From childhood," the distraught father answered. Then the man said, "But if you can do anything, take pity on us and help us" (v.22).

"If you can?" said Jesus. "Everything is possible for him who believes" (v.23)

Immediately the boy's father exclaimed, "I do believe; help me overcome my unbelief!" (v.24).

This statement may seem like a paradox, yet Jesus saw the man's faith and rebuked the evil spirit in the boy, saying, "I command you, come out of him and never enter him again" (v.25).

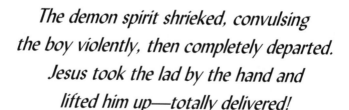

The demon spirit shrieked, convulsing the boy violently, then completely departed. Jesus took the lad by the hand and lifted him up—totally delivered!

FUTURE-SPEAK

Those who don't understand the ways of the Lord have a hard time understanding why we, as born again believers, speak in the present tense of something which is to happen in the future. For example, when Kathy was going through chemotherapy, she declared, "I am healed," even while she still had the symptoms of the illness.

Our God encourages this kind of speaking. He *"calls things that are not as though they were"* (Romans 4:17).

The Lord also works this way regarding your purpose in life. He will plant a seed of faith in your mind and you begin to speak that which does not currently exist. But because this is God's personal vision for you, it is possible to claim it now!

The seed may be tiny and fragile, yet with your confession of the Lord's purpose, it begins to grow. Before long it has been nourished into a viable tree and is producing fruit.

What begins in the spiritual realm becomes physical and tangible.

THE INVISIBLE WORLD

You do not have to visibly see something to possess

it. Scripture declares, *"Now faith is the substance of things hoped for, the evidence of things not seen"* (Hebrews 11:1 KJV).

To put it another way, faith (the "substance") is the basic raw material from which everything is made. It also contains the second ingredient necessary to be real—the evidence of its existence.

This important scripture lets us know that everything is formed in the invisible world (our thoughts, visions and imaginations) before they appear in the physical world. For example:

- Marconi envisioned himself listening to a radio before he invented one.
- Alexander Graham Bell "heard" himself speaking on a telephone before it was created.
- Thomas Edison "saw" the incandescent light bulb before he gave it life.
- Henry Ford pictured thousands of automobiles coming off the assembly line before a factory was ever built.

A God-Given Imagination

Every building, monument, piece of art, business or organization is birthed in the invisible world—as a concept in a person's mind. Then, through talent, leadership and hard work, it comes into being.

————— X —————

I truly believe God's people should be at the forefront of creativity in this world.

After all, we are products of the Creator—and when we are touched by His Spirit, the possibilities are endless.

We have a mandate to help bring God's will into manifestation and should seize every opportunity to take the lead. This is why our young people should become (among other noble professions) teachers, heads of government, international problem solvers and spiritual leaders.

A God-given imagination should operate in harmony with your faith. It gives substance to what you hope for.

THE SOURCE OF EXPECTATION

What I am talking about is not wishful thinking or simply the effects of a positive attitude. No, our anticipation comes from the Father Himself. As the psalmist writes, *"My soul, wait thou only upon God; for my expectation is from him"* (Psalm 62:5 KJV).

How much belief is required for the Lord to turn your

"little" faith into Xtreme Faith? Much less than you think.

Jesus says, *"I tell you the truth, if you have faith as small as a mustard seed, you can say to this mountain, 'Move from here to there' and it will move. Nothing will be impossible for you"* (Matthew 17:20).

What a dynamic combination—faith plus your declaration equals Xtreme Faith!

The Son of God tells us, *"...if two of you on earth agree about anything you ask for, it will be done for you by my Father in heaven"* (Matthew 18:19).

Your words carry divine authority.

IS IT GOD'S WILL?

Faith can be propelled by our imagination, however, we must make certain our creative thoughts are God-produced, not man-induced.

Our thought-processes are important, otherwise the Word would not warn us of their possible misuse. For example, we are told we are to be, *"Casting down imaginations, and every high thing that exalteth itself against the knowledge of God, and bringing into captivity every thought to the obedience of Christ"* (2 Corinthians 10:5 KJV).

Our lives must parallel God's will.

The apostle Paul gives us a few examples of where our minds should be centered: *"Finally, brothers, whatever is true, whatever is noble, whatever is right, whatever is pure, whatever is lovely, whatever is admirable—if anything is excellent or praiseworthy—think about such things"* (Philippians 4:8).

What a different world this would be if God's people would constantly see what is true, noble and worthy of praise!

When you value and nourish what is on the inside—your heart, soul and mind, the Lord will bless you on the outside. As John writes, *"Beloved, I wish above all things that thou mayest prosper and be in health, even as thy soul prospereth"* (3 John 2 KJV).

—————— X —— ——

Your physical well being relies on a soul which is thriving and healthy.

IT'S YOUR CHOICE

Let me offer this warning. Never allow your thoughts and imagination to dwell on carnal desires. The moment such urges surface, prayerfully turn your thoughts elsewhere. Remember, you have been given the power to choose—and you alone make the decision regarding where your mind will be focused.

When our thoughts are linked with the Lord, He will

connect what is natural to what is supernatural and guide us toward His perfect will.

Paul fought a real battle between the flesh and the Spirit. At one point he confessed, *"I know that nothing good lives in me, that is, in my sinful nature. For I have the desire to do what is good, but I cannot carry it out. For what I do is not the good I want to do; no, the evil I do not want to do—this I keep on doing...For in my inner being I delight in God's law; but I see another law at work in the members of my body, waging war against the law of my mind and making me a prisoner of the law of sin at work within my members"* (Romans 7:18-19; 22-23).

What was the answer to this tug-of-war? Paul rejoices, *"...through Christ Jesus the law of the Spirit of life set me free from the law of sin and death"* (Romans 8:2).

SINS OF THE MIND

Jesus addressed the issue of the danger of carnal thoughts when He said, *"You have heard that it was said, 'Do not commit adultery.' But I tell you that anyone who looks at a woman lustfully has already committed adultery with her in his heart* [imagination]" (Matthew 5:27-28).

It is clear by this verse that our thoughts alone are

enough to convict us of sin.

Another of God's commandments is that we should not kill, yet the Word tells us, *"Anyone who hates his brother is a murderer, and you know that no murderer has eternal life in him"* (1 John 3:15).

———— **X** ————

Hate is not a physical act; yet in the invisible realm it is murder.

Never forget that the Word of God is, *"...a discerner of the thoughts and intents of the heart"* (Hebrews 4:12 KJV). And, *"The Lord knows the thoughts of man"* (Psalm 94:11).

SPIRITUAL REVELATIONS

Jesus sent out seventy believers into the harvest field. They returned saying, *"Lord, even the demons submit to us in your name"* (Luke 10:17).

Then He made an amazing statement: *"I saw Satan fall like lightning from heaven"* (v.18).

The Lord wasn't speaking prophetically since the words He used were past tense. He already "saw" an event which would take place more than 2,000 years later. We read in the Book of Revelation, *"The great dragon was hurled down—that ancient serpent called the devil, or Satan, who leads the whole world astray. He was hurled to the earth, and his angels with him"* (Revelation 12:9).

The prince and power of the air is still in the heavenlies, yet Jesus saw him cast down.

———— ✗ ————

The Lord spoke of a future event as if it had already taken place to instruct us as to the importance of visualization in relation to our faith.

Remember, faith is the evidence of things "hoped for." This is why Jesus could see Satan eventually being thrown into the lake of fire (Revelation 20:14).

The vision, wisdom and knowledge God wants us to possess is far beyond human reasoning. *"We demolish arguments and every pretension that sets itself up against the knowledge of God, and we take captive every thought to make it obedient to Christ"* (2 Corinthians 10:5).

Daily, we need to pray for spiritual revelation and guidance so that the very thoughts of God's Son reside in us. As Paul writes, *"Let this mind be in you, which was also in Christ Jesus"* (Philippians 2:5 KJV).

TAUGHT BY THE SPIRIT

As a minister of the Gospel, it saddens me to see people try to obtain the knowledge of God through their own intellect and human reasoning. Timeless truths are imparted to us by the Holy Spirit.

Scripture tells us: *"We have not received the spirit of the world but the Spirit who is from God, that we may understand what God has freely given us. This is what we speak, not in words taught us by human wisdom but in words taught by the Spirit, expressing spiritual truths in spiritual words"* (1 Corinthians 2:12-13).

What you speak must come from heaven.

RE-LIVE THE VICTORIES

Our faith is expanded when we allow our mind to travel in time and space to be witnesses to the events in Bible days:

- We can rejoice with Abraham as God provided a ram to be the substitute sacrifice for Isaac (Genesis 22).
- We can stand on Mount Carmel with Elijah as he called fire down from heaven and defeated the prophets of Baal (1 Kings 18).
- We can see the three Hebrew children as they walked out of the fiery furnace (Daniel 3).

33

- We can be with Paul and Silas as an
  earthquake opened the prison gates and
  they walked out free men (Acts 16).

These victorious events—just by thinking about them—will act to lift our faith, and cause us to believe for miracles today. This is how we can part our own Red Sea and, like Samson, pull down the roof on our enemies. From this moment on, start living in the realm of faith.

CHAPTER THREE

ONLY THE BEST!

Perhaps there's a card in your wallet or purse which gives you entrance into Cosco, Sam's Club or some other members-only warehouse filled to the ceiling with material goods.

I want to let you in on a secret. The moment you asked Christ into your heart, you automatically became an official member of the Heavenly House of Supply. Even more, you didn't have to pay an annual registration fee. Your entrance was a gift—paid once-and-for-all at Calvary.

THE STOREHOUSE IS FULL

In order to fully understand the value of Xtreme Faith, we need to comprehend that God desires us to have total sufficiency in *all* things. This means the Lord has devised a plan to take care of us completely. *"His divine power has given us everything we need for life and godliness through our knowledge of him who called us by his own glory and goodness"* (2 Peter 1:3).

———————X———————

Wow! This tells us we have what we need for "life"—our natural life— and "godliness"—our spiritual life.

When Jesus says, *"I am come that they might have life, and that they might have it more abundantly"* (John 10:10 KJV), He means the shelves of the storehouse are full and running over!

We receive God's provision by faith—which is required for salvation. *"For it is by grace you have been saved, through faith—and this not from yourselves, it is the gift of God"* (Ephesians 2:8).

"BY FAITH"

Hebrews 11 gives us a list of people who received the favor and blessings of God. What was the common denominator?

- *"By faith Noah, when warned about things not yet seen, in holy fear built an ark to save his family"* (Hebrews 11:7).

36

- *"By faith Abraham, when God tested him, offered Isaac as a sacrifice. He who had received the promises was about to sacrifice his one and only son"* (v.17).
- *"By faith Jacob, when he was dying, blessed each of Joseph's sons"* (v.21).
- *"By faith the people* [children of Israel] *passed through the Red Sea as on dry land"* (v.29).

These things were written for two reasons: (1) So we could see how the Lord met their needs and (2) to let us know the Father has a future even greater in store for you and me.

Scripture declares, *"God had planned something better for us so that only together with us would they be made perfect"* (v.40).

This being the case, *"...since we are surrounded by such a great cloud of witnesses, let us throw off everything that hinders and the sin that so easily entangles, and let us run with perseverance the race marked out for us. Let us fix our eyes on Jesus, the author and perfecter of our faith, who for the joy set before him endured the cross, scorning its shame, and sat down at the right hand of the throne of God"* (Hebrews 12:1-2).

Who is the Author and Perfecter of our faith? Jesus Christ.

FAVOR FROM ON HIGH

An incredible supply is waiting with your name attached! What's more, Jesus has an answer for your situation which far exceeds your needs—and this blessing lasts until you step into eternity.

I pray you will allow your faith in God's Word to become so strong that it will erase any doubts and fears concerning your present circumstances.

God's storehouse is waiting for you at this very moment. As Paul writes, *"Praise be to the God and Father of our Lord Jesus Christ, who has blessed us in the heavenly realms with every spiritual blessing in Christ"* (Ephesians 1:3).

WE DON'T HAVE TO WAIT

Yes, our blessings are in the world of the Spirit, yet we have access to them *now*—on this earth—by faith. Remember, *"Every good and perfect gift is from above"* (James 1:17). This does not say these gifts *remain* in heaven, rather they are sent from the Father to us while we serve the Lord.

- God *"...richly provides us with everything for our enjoyment"* (1 Timothy 6:17).

- The Lord will *"...supply and increase your store of seed and will enlarge the harvest of your righteousness. You will be made rich in every way so that you can be generous on every occasion, and through us your generosity will result in thanksgiving to God"* (2 Corinthians 9:10-11).

- Those who follow Christ will receive *"...a hundred times as much in this present age...and in the age to come, eternal life"* (Mark 10:30).

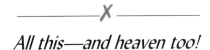

All this—and heaven too!

"SUFFERING FOR JESUS"?

As a loving Father, it is God's responsibility to provide for His children. But, as His children, it is our duty to exercise our faith and receive what is available—to bring these blessings into the natural.

I find it almost impossible to understand how people can have a "suffering for Jesus" mentality when God's Word declares He wants to pour out blessings above and beyond what we are able to receive. As David writes, *"I was young and now I am old, yet I have never seen the righteous forsaken or their children begging bread"* (Psalm 37:25).

I wonder what God must think when He sees one of His children driving down a highway in a rusty, beat-up car with a bumper sticker that proclaims, "I'm a King's Kid!"

———— ✗ ————

The Lord must be grieved when He looks at those who choose to wallow in insufficiency—knowing He paid the ultimate price so we could walk in abundance.

As Scripture tells us, *"For you know the grace of our Lord Jesus Christ, that though he was rich, yet for your sakes he became poor, so that you through his poverty might become rich"* (2 Corinthians 8:9).

Don't hesitate to claim this promise!

YOU'RE AN HEIR!

Make the time to take an inventory of your present situation. How does it relate to the Word? Do you have what you need for *"life and godliness"*—physical and spiritual?

If you are lacking in either of these areas, study the Scriptures and let them speak to your soul. *"All things are yours...the world or life or death or the present or the future—all are yours"* (1 Corinthians 3:21-22).

Thankfully, an increasing number of God's people *are* coming out of their "poverty" mind-set. Yes, as Christians we are to support those in need and help others less fortunate, but how can we give if we have no resources? Without a prosperous church, the Great Commission would be stagnant—and the nations of the world would not be reached for the cause of Christ.

Wouldn't it be wonderful to have enough wealth so you could give 90 percent of your income to the Lord's work and live on the remaining 10 percent?

God is calling us to a higher plane of faith—to accept our place as an heir of the Father and begin enjoying the benefits of His riches.

FROM GLORY TO GLORY

Your path may include hills and valleys, and perhaps there will be times when you don't particularly enjoy the route God allows you to travel. But here is the good news: the road will eventually lead to the summit of the mountain.

The journey is upward—*"...from glory to glory"* (2 Corinthians 3:18).

Don't remain in the past. With great anticipation,

begin to claim His promises for your tomorrow.

Quality Plus Quantity

When the Lord allows you into His storehouse, you will be surprised. It is not a second-hand thrift shop or a consignment outlet. No, from the moment you walk inside you'll see nothing but quality—the absolute finest!

The items you are about to receive are not average or commonplace; they are produced by the Master according to His highest standards. The Bible says, "...*my God shall supply all your need according to His riches in glory by Christ Jesus*" (Philippians. 4:19 KJV).

This means your provisions are not gauged by any earthly comparison, but according to *His* riches. Remember, the Lord is not reaching *into* His supply and seeing it depleted. Rather, He is multiplying what He has and presenting it to you according to His high benchmark.

If you have read my book, *Perpetual Seed —Significant Harvest*, you understand that while the Lord determines the quality of your supply, *you* determine the quantity. Why is this true? Because the amount of your giving determines the amount of what you will receive.

Scripture makes this clear: *"Give, and it will be given to you. A good measure, pressed down, shaken together and running over, will be poured into your lap. For with the measure you use, it will be measured to you"* (Luke 6:38).

————— X —————

*Your actions determine the
answer to "How much?"*

THE SECRET OF THE LORD'S SUPPLY

Many quote the verse, *"God shall supply all your need according to His riches in glory,"* believing it is a universal principle which applies to every Christian regardless of their circumstances.

Take a close look at the context and you'll discover Paul was speaking to the believers at Philippi concerning support for his missionary journeys and spreading the Gospel to the nations.

Specifically, Paul writes, *"...as you Philippians know, in the early days of your acquaintance with the gospel, when I set out from Macedonia, not one church shared with me in the matter of giving and receiving, except you only; for even when I was in Thessalonica, you sent me aid again and again when I was in need. Not that I am looking for a gift, but I am looking for what may be credited to your account. I have received full payment and even more; I am amply supplied, now that I have received from Epaphroditus the gifts you sent. They are a fragrant offering, an acceptable sacrifice, pleasing to God"* (Philippians .4:15-18).

It is only after this admonition that Paul said God would supply all their needs according to His riches in Christ Jesus. In other words, when we faithfully support the work of the Lord, we can expect favor from the Father. He wasn't referring to a one-time gift, rather what they repeatedly sent *"again and again."*

According to this measuring stick, do you qualify to receive the Lord's favor?

BRING OUT THE BEST

Please understand, God takes no pleasure in seeing His children struggling to get by and surviving on substandard goods.

Like the Father of the prodigal son who returned home, the Lord is saying, *"Quick! Bring the best robe and put it on him. Put a ring on his finger and sandals on his feet. Bring the fattened calf and kill it. Let's have a feast and celebrate"* (Luke 15:22-23).

God desires only the finest for His children:

- *"I love those who love me, and those who seek me find me...My fruit is better than fine gold; what I yield surpasses choice silver"* (Proverbs 8:17,19).
- *"The house of the righteous contains great treasure"* (Proverbs 15:6).
- *"If you are willing and obedient, you will eat the best from the land"* (Isaiah 1:19).

When you are faithful and obedient to God's covenants, you will not only have all things, but enjoy the best heaven has to offer.

I pray you are living this abundant, quality life.

CHAPTER FOUR

AN ETERNAL COVENANT

In a place called Haran—which biblical historians locate approximately ten miles north of the Syrian border in present day Turkey—a man named Abraham received a call from God.

The Almighty said, *"Leave your country, your people and your father's household and go to the land I will show you. I will make you into a great nation and I will bless you; I will make your name great, and you will be a blessing...and peoples on earth will be blessed through you"* (Genesis 12:1-3).

By faith, this seventy-five-year-old man and his wife gathered their earthly possessions and headed toward Canaan. When they arrived, God appeared to Abraham again, saying, *"To your offspring I will give this land"* (v.7).

Our "Offspring?"

As the years lengthened, the Lord favored Abraham with great wealth—including livestock, silver and gold (Genesis 12:2). One reason the Lord blessed this man was because he honored God with his giving. Scripture records that he presented Melchizedek (the priestly king) with *"...a tenth of everything"* (Genesis 14:30).

However, there was one matter which concerned Abraham. If the land was to be given to his "offspring," how was this possible since he and his wife, Sarah, were childless?

Abraham reminded the Lord, *"You have given me no children; so a servant in my household will be my heir"* (Genesis 15:3).

God replied, *"This man will not be your heir, but a son coming from your own body will be your heir"* (v.4).

This is when the Almighty took him outside and made an eternal covenant with Abraham. The Lord instructed his servant, *"'Look up at the heavens and count the stars—if indeed you can count them.' Then he said to him, 'So shall your offspring be'"* (v.5). Later, the Lord said, *"I will surely bless you and make your descendants as numerous as the stars in the sky and as the sand on the seashore"* (Genesis 22:17).

SAND AND STARS

This Scripture tells us two different kinds of seed would appear. The first is a natural seed found on the earth (sand of the seashore). The second is like the heavens (the stars of the sky).

In God's Word, the sand of the earth has always symbolized the natural man: *"...the Lord God formed the man from the dust of the ground"* (Genesis 2:7).

————— X —————

The sands of the earth represents Abraham's natural descendants.

However, the Word also tells us, *"The first man was of the dust of the earth, the second man from heaven"* (1 Corinthians 15:47).

The stars are symbolic of the spiritual man—the saints of God. *"Those who are wise will shine like the brightness of the heavens, and those who lead many to righteousness, like the stars for ever and ever"* (Daniel 12:3).

From this point forward, the Almighty gave Abraham two constant reminders of Xtreme Faith—the stars by night and the sandy desert by day.

Today, as believers, you and I are "stars" in God's

covenant: *"If you belong to Christ, then you are Abraham's seed, and heirs according to the promise"* (Galatians 3:29).

A Stranger in the Land

When Abraham and Sarah embarked on their spiritual adventure, their nephew, Lot, was with them. As you study the account, however, there is a distinct difference between the faith of these two men.

Both had been raised in Ur of the Chaldees—a heathen land where the moon-god was worshipped. On their journey, Abraham separated himself from unbelievers: *"By faith he made his home in the promised land like a stranger in a foreign country; he lived in tents"* (Hebrews 11:9). He was *"...looking forward to the city with foundations, whose architect and builder is God"* (v.10).

Lot's Dreadful Decision

The day came when Abraham and Lot parted company and the nephew was given first choice of land to claim for his own.

The Bible chronicles, *"Lot lived among the cities of the plain and pitched his tents near Sodom"* (Genesis 13:12)—whose inhabitants *"...were wicked and were sinning greatly against the Lord"* (v.13).

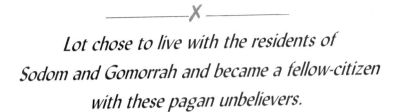

Lot chose to live with the residents of Sodom and Gomorrah and became a fellow-citizen with these pagan unbelievers.

In doing so, Lot failed to separate himself and his family from the world system. This decision also altered Lot's association with the land—his domain became temporary, while Abraham's was forever. As Scripture tells us, *"...we fix our eyes not on what is seen, but on what is unseen. For what is seen is temporary, but what is unseen is eternal"* (2 Corinthians 4:18).

Because of Abraham's deep faith, he was able to pull himself away from the lure of the world.

BURNING RAIN

The influence of the Sodomites affected Lot to such an extent that he lost his moral influence among his own family members. For example, when Lot became convinced God was going to pour down His judgment on Sodom, he *"...went out and spoke to his sons-in-law, who were pledged to marry his daughters. He said, 'Hurry and get out of this place, because the Lord is about to destroy the city!' But his sons-in-law thought he was joking"* (Genesis 19:14).

Lot was right. God *did* bring devastation. Scripture records, *"...the Lord rained down burning sulfur on Sodom and Gomorrah...*[and] *he overthrew those cities and the entire plain, including all those living in the cities—and also the vegetation in the land"* (vv.24-25).

It was a tragic ending.

NEW NAMES

We use the names Abraham and Sarah because that's what most people are familiar with. However, their original names were Abram and Sarai.

When he was 99 years old, God appeared to Abram and made him this promise. He said, *"I will confirm my covenant between me and you and will greatly increase your numbers...You will be the father of many nations. No longer will you be called Abram; your name will be Abraham, for I have made you a father of many nations. I will make you very fruitful; I will make nations of you, and kings will come from you. I will establish my covenant as an everlasting covenant between me and you and your descendants after you for the generations to come"* (Genesis 17:2-7).

Sarai's name was changed too. The Lord told Abraham, *"As for Sarai your wife, you are no longer to call her Sarai; her name will be Sarah. I will bless her and will surely give you a son by her. I will bless her so that she will be the mother of nations; kings of peoples will come from her"* (vv.15-16).

Sarah means "little princess"—quite a name for an elderly woman. However, since she would be the mother of kings, it was certainly appropriate.

WAS THIS A JOKE?

When Abraham heard God say he and Sarah would be parents, he *"...fell facedown; he laughed and said to himself, 'Will a son be born to a man a hundred years old? Will Sarah bear a child at the age of ninety?'"* (v.17).

Later, the Lord spoke to Abraham once more: *"I will surely return to you about this time next year, and Sarah your wife will have a son"* (Genesis 18:10).

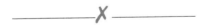

Sarah happened to be standing near the door of the tent and overheard these words.

She couldn't believe what she was hearing: *"Sarah laughed to herself as she thought, 'After I am worn out and my master is old, will I now have this pleasure?'"* (v.11).

God reminded Abraham, *"Is anything too hard for the Lord?"* (v.14).

ALL THINGS NEW

At the time of their name changes, the faith of Abraham and Sarah regarding having a promised son was at a low point—and that's why they made light of the idea. But God was making all things new for this "father of many nations" and his "little princess."

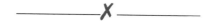

Their desire for each other stirred within them and before long Sarah was pregnant—and into the world came the miracle son—Isaac.

THE BURNT OFFERING

One of the most dramatic stories in Scripture involves the ultimate test of Abraham's faith. God said, *"Take your son, your only son, Isaac, whom you love, and go to the region of Moriah. Sacrifice him there as a burnt offering on one of the mountains I will tell you about"* (Genesis 22:2).

Without one word of complaint or argument, early the next morning, Abraham arose and saddled his donkey. He took with him two of his young servants and his son, Isaac. When he had split enough wood for the burnt offering, he set out for the place God had directed him.

Then, on the third day, when he saw the location in the distance, Abraham said to the servants, *"Stay here with the donkey while I and the boy go over there. We will worship and then we will come back to you"* (v.5).

Abraham asked Isaac to carry the wood, while he took the flint and the knife—and the two of them walked toward the place of sacrifice.

About that time, Isaac asked his father, *"The fire and wood are here...but where is the lamb for the burnt offering?"* (v.7).

Abraham assured him, *"God himself will provide the lamb for the burnt offering, my son"* (v.8).

"ABRAHAM! ABRAHAM!"

When they came to the precise location, Abraham built an altar and put the wood upon it; then he tied up Isaac and laid him on the place of sacrifice. Next, he took out the knife to slay him.

At that exact moment, an angel of the Lord called to him from heaven: "Abraham! Abraham!"

"I am listening," he responded.

"Do not lay a hand on the boy," said the angel. *"Do*

not do anything to him. Now I know that you fear God, because you have not withheld from me your son, your only son" (v.12).

When Abraham looked up, he saw a ram caught by its horns in the thicket. *"He went over and took the ram and sacrificed it as a burnt offering instead of his son"* (v.13).

Abraham named the place appropriately: "The Lord Will Provide."

A SACRED ACT

Centuries later, when the writer of Hebrews refers to this story, we read, *"By faith Abraham, when God tested him, offered Isaac as a sacrifice. He who had received the promises was about to sacrifice his one and only son"* (Hebrews 11:17).

It's important to understand that Abraham wasn't just *willing* to trust God and offer up his son, he actually prepared Isaac for the ultimate sacrifice. What an amazing example of Xtreme Faith!

The Bible has many wonderful things to say concerning the life of Abraham, but they are all based on the fact that he offered his son on the altar. This sacred act was the foundation for all the blessings which followed.

Scripture doesn't tell us Abraham received God's approval when the ram was sacrificed; it was his because of the offering of Isaac.

"By faith" he placed his son on the altar. This tells us Abraham offered Isaac in his *heart*—which was all God needed to see before providing a substitute. Never forget, *"Man looks at the outward appearance, but the Lord looks at the heart"* (1 Samuel 16:7).

NOTHING IS HIDDEN

Even before Abraham raised the knife to follow the Lord's command, in God's sight he had already passed the test.

————— *X* —————

Faith, then, is not an outward act, rather an inward decision.

Abraham was responding to the verbal, spoken Word of the Lord. And today we have the written Word to give us guidance and direction. It, too, knows our inner man. *"For the word of God is living and active. Sharper than any double-edged sword, it penetrates even to dividing soul and spirit, joints and marrow; it judges the thoughts and attitudes of the heart. Nothing in all creation is hidden from God's sight. Everything is uncovered and laid bare before the eyes of him to whom we must give account. Therefore, since we have a great high priest who has gone through the heavens, Jesus the Son of God, let us hold firmly to the faith we profess"* (Hebrews 4:12-14).

ACTING ON THE COVENANT

It is impossible to overstate the depth of Abraham's devotion and faith in God. In his heart of hearts he *knew* Isaac would not die—and even if he did, the Lord would have to raise him from the dead to fulfill the promise that his and Sarah's seed would cover the earth as numerous as the stars in the heavens and the sands of the seashore.

We can recognize Abraham's belief and assurance when he told the two servants, *"Stay here with the donkey while I and the boy go over there. We will worship and then we will come back to you"* (Genesis 22:5).

He didn't say *"I* will return," but *"we"*—meaning Isaac would be with him.

This was more than blind faith of obedience; Abraham was acting on the covenant of God. And it could only be complete if Isaac was spared so that, from his own loins, there would be sons, daughters, grandchildren and the everlasting lineage the Lord promised.

A "COMPLETED" OFFERING

As we read the story, not one drop of Isaac's blood was ever shed on an earthly altar. However, in Abraham's mind he saw the sacrifice taking place.

The offering which was stopped in the natural realm was recorded as "completed" by God Almighty. Why? Because Abraham carried out the command of the Lord in total obedience.

Don't try to second-guess God. There is a reason for His directives, even if you are tested.

Are you ready to enter into an eternal covenant with Him?

CHAPTER FIVE

DECISIONS
IN THE DESERT

After more than 400 years of servitude to the Pharaohs of Egypt, you would think the children of Israel would escape with nothing more than the sandals on their feet and the tattered clothing on their backs. As we will see, this wasn't the case.

When the Jews first arrived in Egypt, *"The descendants of Jacob numbered seventy in all; Joseph was already in Egypt"* (Exodus 1:5).

However, when this generation died, the Bible says, *"...the Israelites were fruitful and multiplied greatly and became exceedingly numerous, so that the land was filled with them"* (v.7).

A new king came to power and was extremely troubled. He warned, *"...the Israelites have become much too numerous for us...we must deal shrewdly with them"* (vv.9-10).

So the king assigned slave masters who forced them into rigorous labor building Pithom and Rameses as supply centers for the king.

But the more they were oppressed, the more they multiplied, *"...so the Egyptians came to dread the Israelites and worked them ruthlessly. They made their lives bitter with hard labor in brick and mortar and with all kinds of work in the fields"* (vv.13-14).

"HURRY! LEAVE!"

After four centuries of oppression, the Almighty used Moses to stand against Pharaoh, demanding, *"This is what the Lord, the God of Israel, says: 'Let my people go'"* (Exodus 5:1).

I know this sounds hard to believe, but the Israelites left Egypt wealthy, not the impoverished people they had been in the past. You see, after nine plagues, Pharaoh couldn't take any more punishment. The tenth, however, was far worse than anything they had experienced—the plague of the firstborn.

God told Moses that on a certain night every firstborn son in Egypt would die. He was to inform the whole community of Israel; the only ones to be spared were those who had sacrificed a lamb and sprinkled the blood on the doorposts. And God said, *"...when I see the blood, I will pass over you"* (Exodus 12:13).

At midnight, *"...the Lord struck down all the firstborn in Egypt, from the firstborn of Pharaoh, who sat on the throne, to the firstborn of the prisoner, who was in the dungeon, and the firstborn of all the livestock as well. Pharaoh and all his officials and all the Egyptians got up during the night, and there was loud wailing in Egypt, for there was not a house without someone dead"* (vv.29-30).

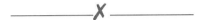

Pharaoh had enough, and told the Jews, "Hurry! Leave this country—otherwise we will all die!"

The Israelites, following Moses' clear instructions, *"...asked the Egyptians for articles of silver and gold and for clothing. The Lord had made the Egyptians favorably disposed toward the people, and they gave them what they asked for; so they plundered the Egyptians"* (vv.35-36).

As a result, the children of Israel began their exodus in wealth instead of poverty.

GRUMBLING CHILDREN

As the days and months progressed—and they moved farther and farther from Egypt—their faith decreased.

Instead of marveling at the miracles, they began to murmur at the circumstances around them.

With increasing volume, they grumbled against Moses and Aaron. They cried, *"If only we had died by the Lord's hand in Egypt! There we sat around pots of meat and ate all the food we wanted, but you have brought us out into this desert to starve this entire assembly to death"* (Exodus 16:3).

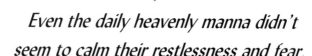

Even the daily heavenly manna didn't seem to calm their restlessness and fear.

God gave Moses the commandments which he read to the people. One law said, *"You shall not make for yourself an idol in the form of anything in heaven above or on the earth beneath or in the waters below"* (Exodus 20:4).

"HIS ANGER BURNED"

In an act of total rebellion, the Israelites collected the gold jewelry they had taken from Egypt and brought it to Aaron—who was complicit in their dissent. The Bible records, *"He took what they handed him and made it into an idol cast in the shape of a calf, fashioning it with a tool. Then they said, 'These are your gods, O Israel, who brought you up out of Egypt'"* (Exodus 32:4).

The next day, the people celebrated with a festival, reveling and making sacrifices to the golden calf.

It was into this decadent scene that Moses came down from the mountain with tablets of the law which God Himself had engraved. *"When Moses approached the camp and saw the calf and the dancing, his anger burned and he threw the tablets out of his hands, breaking them to pieces at the foot of the mountain. And he took the calf they had made and burned it in the fire; then he ground it to powder, scattered it on the water and made the Israelites drink it"* (vv.10-20).

The reason the children of Israel wandered in the desert for forty years and the vast majority of them were not allowed to cross the Jordan with Joshua and Caleb is because of their disobedience and refusal to live by faith.

FAITH IS A CHOICE

I encourage you to read the book of Exodus to see how God gave the people choices—either to obey or to reject His commands. Faith–building miracles were all around them:

- They were led with a cloud by day and a pillar of fire by night (Exodus 13:21:22).

- Bitter waters were sweetened (Exodus 15:25).
- Bread fell from heaven (Exodus 16:13-36).
- Water came out of a rock (Exodus 17:5-8).

We certainly can't blame God for their disobedience —it was their decision.

Often, we quote the Lord's promise to the children of Israel: *"...I will not bring on you any of the diseases I brought on the Egyptians, for I am the Lord, who heals you"* (Exodus 15:26b). However, we overlook the first part of this same scripture: *"If you listen carefully to the voice of the Lord your God and do what is right in his eyes, if you pay attention to his commands and keep all his decrees..."* (v.26a).

Remember, faith without works is dead. If we expect a miracle, we have to "listen," "do," "pay attention" and "keep all His decrees."

A PREVIEW

God allowed the children of Israel to participate in the building of the tabernacle in the wilderness. It was one of the most awesome faith-building endeavors recorded in Scripture.

Even if the people of those days did not realize it's full significance, it is a testimony for us today.

The structure of this tent-like sanctuary allows us to picture many of God's truths:

- The deity of God's Son
- The atonement of Christ
- The judgement of the Almighty
- The heavenlies
- The substitutionary death of Jesus Christ
- The righteousness of the saints
- Witnessing, salvation, the baptism of the Holy Spirit
- The path of the manifested sons into the Holy of Holies
- The body of the born again believers which forms the temple of God today

The tabernacle typified the temple of God in heaven—and the duties of the priests in and around the tabernacle were symbolic of the work our High Priest (Jesus) would one day perform for us in the heavenlies.

The priests, *"...serve at a sanctuary that is a copy and shadow of what is in heaven. This is why Moses was warned when he was about to build the tabernacle: 'See to it that you make everything according to the pattern shown you on the mountain'"* (Hebrews 8:5).

REMINDERS OF RIGHTEOUSNESS

Moses spent forty days and forty nights on Mount Sinai receiving God's plans for this movable sanctuary.

――――――― *X* ―――――――

This invisible tabernacle was brought into reality to give Israel a glimpse of the Lord's coming salvation.

Jesus would not be crucified on the cross until hundreds of years later, yet the event existed in the mind of God in the wilderness.

The children of Israel certainly had opportunities to repent. Every morning when they arose, the tabernacle was the first structure they saw:

- They looked at the linen cloth stretched across the courtyard—a testimony to the righteousness of the saints.
- There were silver-topped pillars— representing the judgment of God.

- Near the entrance was a flock of sacrificial lambs—a type of the Lamb of God who would one day give His life for the sins of the world.

These were reminders, *"...the Lamb slain from the foundation of the world"* (Revelation 13:8 KJV) would one day come and make an eternal atonement.

A CONTINUAL AROMA

A sacrifice of lambs was to be made *"day by day continually"* (Exodus 29:38 KJV)—one lamb in the morning, another in the evening. This was ordained as *"...a pleasing aroma, an offering made to the Lord by fire"* (Numbers 28:6).

What a tangible expression of thanks to the Almighty for His protection in the wilderness. Yet, many chose to reject these reminders their God was with them.

"HOW MUCH MORE?"

Every day, the children of Israel saw the blood on the sacrificial altar. This, however, was just a type and shadow of what was to come.

The blood of the lamb, offered in the Old Testament, was only a temporary covering for sin. Hundreds of years later, a woman named Mary had the faith to believe the Word and conceived a child of the Holy Spirit. This was the long-promised Messiah—God's final solution to the problem of sin.

Scripture reveals that if the blood of animals *"...sprinkled on those who are ceremonially unclean sanctify them so that they are outwardly clean. How much more, then, will the blood of Christ, who through the eternal Spirit offered himself unblemished to God, cleanse our consciences from acts that lead to death, so that we may serve the living God! For this reason Christ is the mediator of a new covenant, that those who are called may receive the promised eternal inheritance— now that he has died as a ransom to set them free from the sins committed under the first covenant"* (Hebrews 9:13-15).

THE FINAL SACRIFICE

Today, you can know this permanent—once-and-for all—redemption. How do you receive Christ? By faith.

If you *"...confess with your mouth, 'Jesus is Lord,' and believe in your heart that God raised him from the dead, you will be saved. For it is with your heart that you believe and are justified, and it is with your mouth that you confess and are saved"* (Romans 10:9-10).

Because of Calvary, you can declare, *"I have been*

crucified with Christ and I no longer live, but Christ lives in me. The life I live in the body, I live by faith in the Son of God, who loved me and gave himself for me" (Galatians 2:20).

The final sacrifice was made with you in mind. By faith, receive the eternal gift your Heavenly Father is offering.

CHAPTER SIX

ANYTHING IS POSSIBLE!

The scene is etched in our memory. A shepherd boy named David places one stone in his slingshot, hurls it, and the mighty Philistine giant, Goliath, falls flat on his face—dead!

However, what took place after this dramatic encounter is equally important. The day marked the end of Goliath's victories, but it was a new dawning for the young conquering hero.

After Goliath was slain with a well-aimed stone which sank deep into his forehead, David rushed up, pulled Goliath's sword from its sheath and cut off the giant's head.

You can imagine the fear this struck into the hearts of the Philistines. The Bible says, *"...the men of Israel and Judah surged forward with a shout and pursued the Philistines to the entrance of Gath and to the gates of*

Ekron. Their dead were strewn along the Shaaraim road to Gath and Ekron" (v.52).

THEY WERE TERRIFIED

Where was David? He *"...took the Philistine's head and brought it to Jerusalem"* (v.54).

—————— ✗ ——————

This was much more than a trophy. It was a symbol to the Israelites that if you have faith, you can defeat any foe.

After all, the mighty Philistines had been the arch-enemy of Judah for years, and the Jewish soldiers shuddered at the thought of fighting them.

During the standoff, before David boldly faced the giant, King Saul's forces cowered in the presence of the enemy. When Goliath issued a challenge for one man to step forward and face him, *"On hearing the Philistine's words, Saul and all the Israelites were dismayed and terrified"* (v.11).

So here was David, parading the head of the giant though the streets of Jerusalem, proclaiming, "Why should we fear? When God is with us, anything is possible!"

"WHOSE SON ARE YOU?"

King Saul only knew David as the person who played the harp to ease his mental suffering when he felt despondent. Remember, *"...the Spirit of the Lord had departed from Saul, and an evil spirit from the Lord tormented him"* (1 Samuel 16:15).

Saul didn't know that the high priest, Samuel, had been directed by God Himself to find a replacement for the king—and the youngest son from the house of Jesse had been chosen and anointed as the future leader of Israel.

Saul became curious and asked the commander of his army, Abner, to bring David before him. When the giant-slayer arrived, he was *"...still holding the Philistine's head"* (v.57).

"Whose son are you, young man?" Saul asked him.

David replied, *"I am the son of your servant Jesse of Bethlehem"* (v.58).

A JEALOUS KING

Suddenly, the loyalty and confidence of the Israelites was shifting from Saul to David. In the streets there were huge celebrations.

When the soldiers marched back from the battle,

"...the women came out from all the towns of Israel to meet King Saul with singing and dancing, with joyful songs and with tambourines and lutes. As they danced, they sang: 'Saul has slain his thousands, and David his tens of thousands'" (1 Samuel 18:6-7).

What a slap in the face for Saul! He became extremely angry: *"'They have credited David with tens of thousands,' he thought, 'but me with only thousands. What more can he get but the kingdom?'"*

———— X ————

From that day forward, Saul was increasingly jealous of David and watched him constantly.

Yet, the people lauded the young man so much that Saul had no other choice but to name him a commander of the army, and, *"In everything he did he had great success, because the Lord was with him"* (v.14).

WHERE IS YOUR TRUST?

David's eventual rise to the throne is a chronicle of Xtreme Faith—inwardly knowing the same God who allowed him to defeat the giant would never leave him nor forsake him.

David was later able to write: *"Some trust in chariots*

and some in horses, but we trust in the name of the Lord our God" (Psalm 20:7).

When you have the battle-tested faith of David, you, too, will be able to declare:

- *"Lord, You are my Shepherd"* (Psalm 23:1).
- *"I will no longer be in need"* (v.1).
- *"You lead me beside still waters"* (v.2).
- *"You restore my soul"* (v.3).
- *"You guide me in paths of righteousness"* (v.3).
- *"Even though I walk through the valley of the shadow of death, I will fear no evil"* (4).
- *"You are with me—Your rod and staff comfort me"* (v.4).
- *"You prepare a banquet for me in the presence of my enemies"* (v.5).
- *"You anoint my head with oil"* (v.5).
- *"My cup overflows with blessing"* (v.5).
- *"Your goodness and love will follow me all the days of my life"* (v.6).
- *"I will dwell in Your house forever"* (v.6).

Praise the Lord!

THE PROPHET'S CHAMBER

Have you ever noticed how faith inspires faith? When

you trust and believe, it creates an atmosphere of hope and expectation.

David had a tremendous impact on the faith of Solomon. And before their time, Elijah instilled belief into Elisha—and in turn, he touched many lives.

During the journeys of the prophet Elisha, he often passed through a place called Shunem—a small village on a hill in a region later known as Galilee.

One of the reasons he stopped there so often was because of the hospitality of a certain woman and her husband. It became a custom for him to drop in for a meal whenever he was in the area.

After several visits, the woman suggested to her husband, *"I know that this man who often comes our way is a holy man of God. Let's make a small room on the roof and put in it a bed and a table, a chair and a lamp for him. Then he can stay there whenever he comes to us"* (2 Kings 4:9-10).

SHE WAS STUNNED!

On his next journey through Shunem, Elisha used the room to sleep and rest. Then he said to his servant, Gehazi, "Tell the woman I would like to speak with her."

Standing in the doorway, she was told, *"You have gone to all this trouble for us. Now what can be done for you? Can we speak on your behalf to the king or the commander of the army?"* (v.13).

She replied, "I am perfectly happy and satisfied with my life."

Elisha turned to his servant and said, "Surely there must be something we can do for her. What would it be?"

Gehazi thought for a moment and said, *"Well, she has no son and her husband is old"* (v.14).

Immediately, God inspired Elisha to give her this prophecy: *"About this time next year...you will hold a son in your arms"* (v.16).

She was stunned! *"'No, my lord,' she objected. 'Don't mislead your servant, O man of God!'"* (v.16).

Well, the woman conceived, and just as Elisha had said, she bore a son.

CALL 911?

The child grew, and one day while he was working in a harvest field with his father, he began to complain, "My head! My head!"

Quickly, the dad ordered a servant to carry the boy to

his mother. About noon, laying on her lap, he died.

In an emergency situation like this, most moms would call 911 and rush the boy to a hospital. Not this woman!

Suddenly, faith began to rise within her. She knew the prophet of God had power with the Almighty—and she needed that power more than any other time in her life.

Even though her son had died in her lap, she refused to accept what the death messenger had sent.

With the boy cradled in her arms, she recalled the times Elisha had slept in the bed upstairs. So she carefully carried her son there, placed him on the bed, and shut the door.

Next, she told her husband, *"Please send me one of the servants and a donkey so I can go to the man of God quickly and return"* (v.22).

"Why go to him today?" he asked—not knowing his son had died.

The Shunammite woman then claimed his healing with this positive confession. She said to her husband, *"It's all right"* (v.23).

What a powerful statement of faith!

She Wouldn't Let Go

With the utmost urgency, she saddled one of the donkeys and ordered her servant, *"Lead on; don't slow down for me unless I tell you"* (v.24).

As she approached Mount Carmel, Elisha recognized her in the distance and knew something must be wrong. So he told Gehazi to run and meet her and ask, *"Are you all right? Is your husband all right? Is your child all right?"* (v.26).

Once more, the woman claimed healing for her son, declaring by faith, *"Everything is all right"* (v.26).

———— X ————

When she finally reached Elisha at the mountain, she threw herself at his feet and simply wouldn't let go.

Gehazi came over to pull her away, but the man of God said, *"Leave her alone! She is in bitter distress, but the Lord has hidden it from me and has not told me why"* (v.27).

"TAKE MY STAFF"

In the presence of the prophet, the woman's faith did not falter. She asked him, *"Did I ask you for a son, my lord?...Didn't I tell you, 'Don't raise my hopes'?"* (v.28).

In that moment, Elisha knew the son had died. So he told Gehazi, *"Tuck your cloak into your belt, take my staff in your hand and run. If you meet anyone, do not greet him, and if anyone greets you, do not answer. Lay my staff on the boy's face"* (v.29).

Gehazi and the woman ran back to her home with a point of contact—the prophet's staff. This kept her faith alive!

On entering the home, Gehazi ran upstairs and placed the staff on the boy's face, but there was no response. This spark of faith ignited into flame when Elisha reached the home.

THE BOY SNEEZED!

When he walked in, the boy was lying on the bed with no signs of life. Scripture records, *"He went in, shut the door on the two of them and prayed to the Lord. Then he got on the bed and lay upon the boy, mouth to mouth, eyes to eyes, hands to hands. As he stretched himself out upon him, the boy's body grew warm. Elisha turned away and walked back and forth in the room and then got on the bed and stretched out upon him once more. The boy sneezed seven times and opened his eyes"* (vv.33-35).

The prophet called his servant and said, "Bring the Shunammite woman here." There was great rejoicing because her son was brought back to life.

THE HAND OF GOD

In no way am I telling you to avoid medical help in crisis situations, but I want you to understand that God honors Xtreme Faith.

If you'll take a moment to reflect, perhaps there have been times in your own life when you faced a circumstance which seemed impossible—a health problem, a financial dilemma or a shattered relationship. Looking back, you can now see the hand of God working on your behalf.

What the Lord did for you then, He will do for you now! By faith, the giants in your life will be destroyed—and God's power will restore you once gain.

You will shout, "Hallelujah!"

CHAPTER SEVEN

SWEPT CLEAN!

To live and experience the level of faith God requires of His children demands an internal house-cleaning. We need to remove the clutter of culture, the confinement of tradition and the hypocrisy of man-made religion.

Scripture records how Jesus cleansed the temple, yet His actions were not only to demonstrate God's disgust with what was taking place in the synagogue, but also in the heart and soul of man.

"WHO IS THIS?"

In Matthew, Mark and Luke we read the account of Jesus' entrance into Jerusalem just before His arrest, trial and crucifixion.

The Lord asked the disciples to go into a village and find a donkey with a colt beside her. This was in direct fulfillment of the prophecy God spoke through Zechariah, *"Rejoice greatly, O Daughter of Zion! Shout,*

Daughter of Jerusalem! See, your king comes to you, righteous and having salvation, gentle and riding on a donkey, on a colt, the foal of a donkey" (Zechariah 9:9).

Rejoice indeed!

———————X———————

When Jesus came riding into the city on a donkey—the picture of humility —a large crowd assembled.

The Bible says they, *"....spread their cloaks on the road, while others cut branches from the trees and spread them on the road. The crowds that went ahead of him and those that followed shouted, 'Hosanna to the Son of David!' 'Blessed is he who comes in the name of the Lord!' 'Hosanna in the highest!'"* (Matthew 21:8-9).

Then, as Jesus entered the city, it caused considerable commotion. The people asked, "Who is this?"

The crowds following Him answered, *"This is Jesus, the prophet from Nazareth in Galilee"* (v.11).

Immediately, Jesus headed straight for the temple area and drove out all who were buying and selling there—and He overturned the money changers and the benches of those hawking merchandise.

In a loud voice, He declared, *"It is written... 'My*

house will be called a house of prayer,' but you are making it a 'den of robbers'" (v.13).

SCATTERED COINS

The book of John, however, records another cleansing of the temple—which occurred much earlier in the ministry of Jesus.

Just after the first miracle of the Son of God (turning water into wine at the marriage celebration in Cana), Jesus journeyed to Jerusalem. It was during the time the Jewish Passover was being observed.

What He saw there astonished Him. *"In the temple courts he found men selling cattle, sheep and doves, and others sitting at tables exchanging money. So he made a whip out of cords, and drove all from the temple area, both sheep and cattle; he scattered the coins of the money changers and overturned their tables"* (John 2:14-15).

To those who sold the doves, He ordered, *"Get these out of here! How dare you turn my Father's house into a market!"* (v.16).

His disciples remembered that it was written, "...[the] *zeal for your house consumes me"* (Psalm 69:9).

A RESURRECTED TEMPLE

The religious leaders demanded, *"What miraculous*

sign can you show us to prove your authority to do all this?" (John 2:18).

Jesus answered them, *"Destroy this temple, and I will raise it again in three days"* (v.19).

The Jews replied, *"It has taken forty-six years to build this temple, and you are going to raise it in three days?"* (v. 20).

Jesus, however, was referring to His own body as the temple (v.21). Much later, after the resurrection, His disciples recalled hearing Him give the "three days" prophecy.

IS IT A WORTHY PLACE?

When God's Son entered the temple in Jerusalem to purify it, He was not speaking of a holy site made of stone—which the religious leaders had desecrated. Instead, Jesus was telling the people of His day—and you and me—how our bodies, the temple of flesh, must be made pure and righteous.

The message being: we are to be tough on ourselves and conquer every wrong thought and sinful perversion. We must overturn the tables of our self-centered lives and chase out Satan's influence over our spirit. Plus, God wants us to build barriers to block out intruders who would try every which way to destroy us.

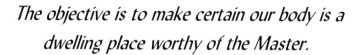

The objective is to make certain our body is a dwelling place worthy of the Master.

As the apostle Paul writes: *"Do you not know that your bodies are members of Christ himself?"* (1 Corinthians 6:15).

TAKE A STAND!

Some people ask, "If Jesus said we are to be meek, why did He become angry and drive the moneychangers out of the temple?"

Jesus was stern regarding God's house because it was an extension of His Father's work on earth. Certainly He was humble and patient, yet there were certain standards of conduct He would not tolerate.

There are situations in our own lives when we are required to take a stand between right and wrong, yet having done so on principle, we must love those we have corrected. For example, just after this event, Jesus shared the message of redemption with Nicodemus, a member of the Jewish ruling council. He explained to the man why, *"God so loved the world..."* (John 3:16).

Jesus demonstrated both His strength and grace.

"LIVING SACRIFICES"

By His actions, Jesus shows us we need to continually free ourselves from any filth or dirt in our personal temples. This may take place through the washing by the Word (Ephesians 5:26). In Scripture, the Word is often referred to as "water."

At other times, we need to go into our inner temple and correct any mistakes through self-discipline. We can't simply allow the vendors of evil—whether deceit, lust or carnality—to operate in or through us.

You and I have the personal responsibility for keeping our "inner man" clean. Scripture counsels, *"...offer your bodies as living sacrifices, holy and pleasing to God—this is your spiritual act of worship"* (Romans 12:1).

One of the reasons Paul became a powerful messenger of the Gospel was his self-discipline. He wrote to the believers at Corinth, *"I keep under my body and bring it into subjection: lest that by any means, when I have preached to others, I myself should be a castaway"* (1 Corinthians 9:27 KJV).

WHO WILL FILL THE VOID?

Likewise, we are taught to cleanse our heart so as to make it pleasing and hospitable for the Lord's presence.

However, if you sweep out sin, yet do not allow God to take up residence, you'll soon be back where you started—perhaps even worse. The devil will rush in to fill the void.

Here is what Jesus told the religious scholars and Pharisees: *"When an evil spirit comes out of a man, it goes through arid places seeking rest and does not find it. Then it says, 'I will return to the house I left.' When it arrives, it finds the house unoccupied, swept clean and put in order. Then it goes and takes with it seven other spirits more wicked than itself, and they go in and live there. And the final condition of that man is worse than the first. That is how it will be with this wicked generation"* (Matthew 12:43-45).

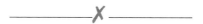

The most effective way I know to keep Satan out and not allow him any leeway in our lives is to be filled—and stay filled with the Holy Spirit.

"TAKE HEART!"

I get excited when I think that, even before Jesus went to the cross to rid my life of sin, He saw the work as completed.

One of the most powerful statements ever made by

the Lord is when He said, *"In this world you will have trouble. But take heart! I have overcome the world"* (John 16:33).

Since this was *before* His crucifixion, why did He phrase a future event as if it had already occurred?

While on earth, Jesus possessed a spiritual mentality—the ability to think as God thinks. This is why He called things which were not as though they were.

At this particular juncture, Jesus knew He was leaving and the disciples would be scattered. He also saw their faith beginning to weaken, so He encouraged His followers, "Take heart! I have overcome the world!"

This is why He spoke of victory over death, hell and the grave as events which had already taken place.

New Thoughts

In reality, only a few days later, we find Christ hanging on the cross at Calvary—being ridiculed, reviled, beaten and killed. Then He was sealed in a borrowed tomb.

Yet, He *had* overcome, and the disciples would see the manifestation of the risen Christ.

As a believer, on the authority of God's Word, you have the right to declare you have a clean heart and a temple of clay which is pure because it has been washed in the precious blood of the Lamb.

Why can you speak confidently of these things? Because you take the Word seriously when it says, *"Let this mind be in you, which was also in Christ Jesus"* (Philippians 2:5 KJV).

Suddenly, you have a new way of thinking. The Lord says, *"For my thoughts are not your thoughts, neither are your ways my ways"* (Isaiah 55:8).

By faith, you can present your body "pure and spotless" before the Lord, knowing it is not your righteousness, but His, which has made you clean.

This makes me want to rejoice and shout— Hallelujah!

CHAPTER EIGHT

"I WAS BLIND, BUT NOW I SEE!"

Xtreme Faith can surface from the most unlikely sources. For example, Jesus used His saliva mixed with the dust of the earth in the healing of a man who was blind from birth.

Picture the scene. Jesus had just left a pressure-filled confrontation with the Jewish leaders over His authority to speak on God's behalf. The atmosphere was so tense, *"...they picked up stones to stone him, but Jesus hid himself, slipping away from the temple grounds"* (John 8:59).

The encounter didn't seem to bother the Lord. In fact, He was calm and composed as He journeyed on with His disciples.

Obviously, Jesus wasn't dwelling on the matter, because the Bible says, *"As he went along, he saw a man blind from birth"* (John 9:1).

At this point, the disciples asked the Lord, *"Rabbi, who sinned, this man or his parents, that he was born blind?"* (v.2).

Jesus answered, *"Neither this man nor his parents sinned...but this happened so that the work of God might be displayed in his life"* (v.3).

THE LIGHT OF THE WORLD

This was not a random meeting, but one which was planned and prepared by the Almighty to confirm the Word and bolster faith and belief.

Here was an opportunity to demonstrate to the critics that Jesus truly was the Messiah. This is made clear as He tells the disciples, *"As long as it is day, we must do the work of him who sent me. Night is coming, when no one can work. While I am in the world, I am the light of the world"* (vv.4-5).

The healing which was about to take place testifies to the fact that Jesus came to bring both spiritual and physical light to the blind. The previous day, He told His accusers, *"I am the light of the world. Whoever follows me will never walk in darkness, but will have the light of life"* (John 8:12).

Now, with the sightless man before Him, Jesus, *"...spit on the ground, made some mud with the saliva, and put it on the man's eyes"* (John 9:6).

Next, the Lord told him to go wash in the Pool of Siloam. (It is interesting to note this same pool has recently been rediscovered and is located at the lowest point in Jerusalem. It was a freshwater reservoir and a major gathering place for Jews making pilgrimages to the city.)

What happened next? Scripture records, *"So the man went and washed, and came home seeing"* (v.7).

Praise the Lord!

DOUBLY BLIND!

The method Jesus used was unusual. In healing services today, we follow the admonition of James 5:14-15 and anoint a person with oil, praying the prayer of faith.

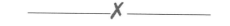

In this case, Jesus took the mud and literally smeared it on the blind man.

The Amplified Bible says, *"He spread it [as ointment] on the man's eyes"* (v.6).

He was now *doubly* blind—first from his physical condition, and now from the mask of clay which was covering him.

I believe this man's faith began to escalate with every step he took toward the Pool of Siloam. He could hardly wait to wash off the mud and see the rays of the sun for the first time in his life.

———— X ————

The man's faith was richly rewarded.
Jesus had healed him!

"I AM THE MAN"

His friends and neighbors—and those who had seen him asking for alms, asked, *"Isn't this the same man who used to sit and beg?"* (v.8).

Shocked at the very idea he could now see, some doubted, *"No, he only looks like him"* (v.9).

But the beggar insisted, "I am the man."

"How did this happen?" they wanted to know.

He replied, *"The man they call Jesus made some mud and put it on my eyes. He told me to go to Siloam and wash. So I went and washed, and then I could see"* (v.11).

Curious, they inquired, "Where is He?"

"I don't know," the healed beggar answered.

Looking for Details

The word spread quickly and the Pharisees called for the one who had been blind—looking for any reason to accuse Jesus.

The day on which the healing took place was a Sabbath, so the religious leaders wanted to document the event. They asked the man for details and he told them, *"He put mud on my eyes...and I washed, and now I see"* (v.15).

Some of the Pharisees commented, *"'This man is not from God, for he does not keep the Sabbath.' But others asked, 'How can a sinner do such miraculous signs?' So they were divided"* (v.16).

Finally they questioned the blind man, *"What have you to say about him? It was your eyes he opened"* (v.17).

The beggar replied, "He is a prophet."

"You'll Have to Ask Him"

The Pharisees still weren't convinced he had truly been blind and received his sight, so they sent for his parents.

"Is this your son?" they wanted to know. *"Is this the one you say was born blind? How is it that now he can see?"* (v.19).

The mother and father assured them, "We know he is our son, and we also can tell you with absolute truth that he was born blind."

Then his parents added, "How it is that he can see or who opened his eyes, we don't know. You'll have to ask him. He is of age and can speak for himself."

The reason they hesitated to give too much information is because they were afraid of the religious authorities, *"...for already the Jews had decided that anyone who acknowledged that Jesus was the Christ would be put out of the synagogue"* (v.22).

BEYOND ARGUMENT

For a second time, the Pharisees, summoned the man who had been blind. "Why don't you give glory to God?" they asked him. "We know this man Jesus is just an impostor."

He replied that he didn't know whether or not this was true. Then he stated, *"One thing I do know. I was blind but now I see!"* (v.25).

I've heard it quoted, "A man with an experience is never at the mercy of a man with an argument."

This guy nailed it! He didn't care what the critics said because he could see!

THEY THREW HIM OUT

The Pharisees still weren't finished. They persisted, *"What did he do to you? How did he open your eyes?"* (v.26).

Exasperated, he answered, *"I have told you already and you did not listen. Why do you want to hear it again? Do you want to become his disciples, too?"* (v.27).

That did it! The Pharisees began to hurl insults at him saying, *"You are this fellow's disciple! We are disciples of Moses! We know that God spoke to Moses, but as for this fellow, we don't even know where he comes from"* (vv.28-29).

The former blind man answered, *"Now that is remarkable! You don't know where he comes from, yet he opened my eyes. We know that God does not listen to sinners. He listens to the godly man who does his will. Nobody has ever heard of opening the eyes of a man born blind. If this man were not from God, he could do nothing"* (vv.30-33).

To this the Pharisees replied, *"You were steeped in sin at birth; how dare you lecture us!"* (v.34). And they threw him out!

"Lord, I Believe"

Jesus heard how badly the religious leaders had treated the man and when He found him, asked, *"Do you believe in the Son of Man?"* (v.35).

"Who is He, Sir?" the beggar inquired. "Tell me so that I may believe in him."

Jesus said, *"You have now seen him; in fact, he is the one speaking with you"* (v.37). To which the man exclaimed, "Lord, I believe;" and he worshipped Him.

Amazing Grace

Jesus used the opportunity to show the contrast of what will happen to those who believe versus those who refuse. He said, *"For judgment I have come into this world, so that the blind will see and those who see will become blind"* (v.39).

Some Pharisees who had followed Jesus to the meeting and overheard Him uttering these words, asked, *"What? Are we blind too?"* (v.40).

Jesus answered, *"If you were blind, you would not be guilty of sin; but now that you claim you can see, your guilt remains"* (v.41).

Sight—both natural and supernatural—comes from faith, not from logic, reasoning or religious tradition. I pray you can sing the words of Amazing Grace from your soul:

I once was lost, but now am found,
Was blind, but now I see.

THE PERFUME

During the final days before Christ had to go to the cross, He did all He could so the faith of the disciples would remain strong during this difficult time.

While the high priests and religious leaders were looking for a way to seize Jesus and kill Him, He was in Bethany, a guest in the home of Simon the Leper.

During a meal, while Jesus was seated at the table, *"...a woman came with an alabaster jar of very expensive perfume...She broke the jar and poured the perfume on his head"* (Mark 14:3).

Several who were present became indignant saying to one another, *"Why this waste of perfume? It could have been sold for more than a year's wages and the money given to the poor"* (vv.4-5).

When they harshly rebuked the woman, Jesus interrupted, *"Why are you bothering her? She has done a beautiful thing to me. The poor you will always have with you, and you can help them any time you want. But you will not always have me. She did what she could. She poured perfume on my body beforehand to prepare for my burial. I tell you the truth, wherever the gospel is preached throughout the world, what she has done will also be told, in memory of her"* (vv.6-9).

ON SCHEDULE

This was such an unusual act—anointing a person for burial before the person had actually died. Yet, Jesus did not stop what the woman was doing.

By commending her, Jesus was letting those present know His death was truly imminent and He wanted to especially imprint this fact on the minds of the disciples.

———— X ————

It was to tell them once more that God's plan was on schedule, and what He had told them during three years of ministry was about to take place.

This was to fortify their faith. Yet, we know that at the crucifixion their spirits practically collapsed, and they traveled through a dark valley before finally seeing the risen Christ.

All of these events served a purpose, and the seeds of

belief which were planted eventually took root.

PRAYING FOR A PARALYTIC

The lessons of faith taught by Jesus remained with the disciples long after the Lord ascended back to the Father.

For example, when Peter went on a mission to visit the churches that had been established in the name of Christ, he arrived at a city called Lydda and met with the believers. And while he was there, Peter met a man named Aeneas—a paralytic who had been bedridden eight years.

With total faith in the miracle-working power of the Lord, Peter said to the man, *"Jesus Christ heals you. Get up and take care of your mat"* (Acts 9:34).

Immediately Aeneas jumped out of that bed!

"PLEASE COME AT ONCE!"

The news of this healing circulated quickly. And down the road in Joppa there was a believer named Tabitha (translated Dorcas). She was known throughout the city for her good deeds and helping the poor.

Tragically, the woman became sick and died. Her body was prepared for burial and she *"...was washed and placed in an upstairs room"* (v.37).

Members of the church heard Peter was in Lydda and

sent two men to ask if he could come to Joppa. They urged him, *"Please come at once!"* (v.38).

Peter left immediately and went with the men—and they led him to the upstairs room where the woman's body was laid out. As Scripture describes the scene: *"All the widows stood around him, crying and showing him the robes and other clothing that Dorcas* [Tabitha] *had made while she was still with them"* (v.39).

Her sewing skills were not important to Peter. He demanded that all of the widows leave the room, then he knelt and prayed. Next, he turned to the dead woman and commanded in the name of Jesus, *"Tabitha, get up"* (v.40).

"SIGNS FOLLOWING"

It's important to note that Peter didn't walk into the upper chamber and first look at the corpse. Instead he prayed—allowing faith to stir within him to the point he was ready to view the dead body and believe for a miracle.

The Word of God records that the woman opened her eyes, and when she saw Peter, sat up. *"He took her by the hand and helped her to her feet. Then he called the believers and the widows and presented her to them alive"* (v.41).

As you can imagine, in this small fishing village, the

report of Tabitha's healing spread like wildfire.

What was the result? The Bible says, *"...many people believed in the Lord"* (v.42).

Once again, faith brought about a miracle—and the miracle caused the church to grow and flourish.

Today, the "signs following" that were promised to believers before Jesus returned to heaven (Mark 16:17) are available to you and me.

In addition to physical healing and spiritual deliverance, those who are dead in trespasses and sin can be made alive—and those who are blinded by this world can receive sight!

Christ is still the Light of the World!

CHAPTER NINE

FAITH THAT MULTIPLIES

Long before CNN, NBC, USA Today or the Internet, news still traveled at amazing speed. One person told another, and before long entire cities and nations were aware of what was taking place around them and beyond.

In Jesus' day, people everywhere seemed to know about Him. They had heard through the grapevine of the incredible miracles He performed—such as healing the son of the Roman centurion (John 4:43-54) and the invalid laying beside the Pool of Bethesda who suddenly began to walk (John 5:1-18).

THE "BREAD" DILEMMA

Shortly after these events, Jesus crossed the Sea of Galilee and was surprised to see a huge crowd awaiting

His arrival. He tried to find a quiet place to rest, walking up on a hillside with His disciples.

The throng could not be stopped and they quickly followed Him.

In this remote area, Jesus looked at Philip and asked, *"Where shall we buy bread for these people to eat?"* (John 6:5).

Actually, the Lord only voiced this question to test Philip, because He knew exactly what He was going to do (v.6). Jesus was letting His disciples know that to feed a crowd of this magnitude, a human solution was highly unlikely.

Philip, thinking in the natural, answered Him, *"Eight months' wages would not buy enough bread for each one to have a bite!"* (v. 7).

BEYOND LOGICAL THOUGHT

In this story we find two distinct patterns of thinking at work—the natural mind and the supernatural—and it is easy to spot the difference.

The problem was enormous. The thousands of hungry people needed to be fed and it was a long distance to walk to the city and eat.

Philip's view of the situation was typical of the average human logical thought process. To find a solution, he reached into his analytical mind.

Unfortunately, this reasoning only considered what was practical and visible. When this happens, we often look for reasons to fail rather than to succeed.

His finite mind was stymied by the obstacles—and he was unable to see past them.

When Philip suggested that two months' wages would *"not be enough"* he was already admitting defeat. What faith-destroying words! Yet they are typical of millions who see problems instead of possibilities, difficulties rather than deliverance.

———— *X* ————

The longer we are exposed to such negative thinking the more it permeates our spirit.

As a result, we fall into Satan's clutches of hopelessness and despair.

We need to realize the Lord desires that we have *"...sufficiency in all things"* (2 Corinthians 9:8 KJV).

"WHAT'S THE USE?"

Then, Andrew, Simon Peter's brother, spoke up saying, *"Here is a boy with five small barley loaves and two small fish"* (John 6:9).

At last, a glimmer of hope compared to the negativity

of Philip. Andrew had an inkling of what Jesus could do with a few loaves of bread and two fish. His response was much like Mary, the mother of Jesus, at the wedding in Cana. She said, *"Do whatever he tells you"* (John 2:4).

Andrew's very words show us he was more concerned with what they *had,* they what they *lacked.*

Philip was saying, "What's the use? All our money put together wouldn't buy enough bread for this crowd." But Andrew, looking at the exact same problem, saw the possibility that perhaps—just perhaps—Jesus could do something with a young boy's lunch.

———— *X* ————

Andrew knew what the Master could do. After all, he had seen Him make wine from water!

Was his faith being tested? Of course. Andrew was probably influenced by Philip when, after telling Jesus about the loaves and fish, added, *"...but what are they among so many?"* (John 6:9).

Yet, Andrew believed.

"WHATEVER WE ASK"

The solution of Philip to pool resources and purchase a vast amount of bread had some merit—at least it would demonstrate to the throng they were concerned. However, he knew their best efforts would still be insufficient.

Those who choose to walk by faith don't necessarily have to be unrealistic. However, they have made the decision to walk in a realm of the Spirit which is always far and above average. This is why we call it Xtreme Faith.

We speak the Word, which declares, *"This is the confidence we have in approaching God: that if we ask anything according to his will, he hears us. And if we know that he hears us—whatever we ask—we know that we have what we asked of him"* (1 John 5:14-15).

THE BOY DIDN'T HESITATE

In addition to Jesus, there were at least two others who had faith this lad's lunch could be the answer to the food problem—Andrew, and the boy himself. Otherwise, the young man would not have volunteered to give what he had brought to eat.

The boy somehow sensed Andrew had power with the Lord since he was a disciple of Jesus. This is why he didn't hesitate to place his lunch in the hand of a man of God.

Friend, be careful where you plant your offering. Pray for guidance and make certain it is sown into good, fertile ground.

HE GAVE THANKS

The events which followed were primarily for the benefit of the disciples. It was the perfect situation to teach them how to stretch their faith for the impossible.

Jesus turned to them and said, *"Have the people sit down"* (John 6:10).

The Bible records there were about 5,000 men (v.10). Since this number didn't include the women and children, some biblical scholars estimate the crowd to have been between 10,000 and 15,000 people. Now that's a lot of hungry mouths to feed!

Jesus then took the bread, and after giving thanks, gave it to those who were seated—as much as they wanted. He did the same with the fish.

When Jesus prayed over the meager provisions, He no doubt thanked His Father for both the faith of the lad and that of Andrew for bringing the lunch to Him. It was one more demonstration of agreement: *"Again, I tell you that if two of you on earth agree about anything you ask for, it will be done for you by my Father in heaven"* (Matthew 18:19).

"PIECE BY PIECE"

When the crowd had satisfied their hunger, Jesus said

to His disciples, *"Gather the pieces that are left over. Let nothing be wasted"* (John 6:12).

After collecting the remainder from the original five barley loaves, they filled twelve baskets!

Remember, it was Jesus who broke apart what was in the basket—then He passed it out to the disciples who distributed it to those present.

Some have wondered how this actually took place. Did God simply open the windows of heaven and pour down tons of fish and thousands of loaves of bread and have them land in a big pile on the side of that mountain? No, Jesus gave the food out piece by piece—yet the content of the basket was never exhausted.

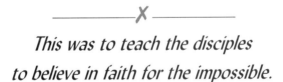

This was to teach the disciples to believe in faith for the impossible.

Obviously, the message the Lord was demonstrating was not lost.

When Jesus was taken up into heaven, *"...the disciples went out and preached everywhere, and the Lord worked with them and confirmed his word by the signs that accompanied it"* (Mark 16:20).

This was a united effort:

- As believers began to spread the Gospel, *"The Lord's hand was with them, and a great number of people believed and turned to the Lord"* (Acts 11:21).
- The Lord sent the disciples out two by two (Mark 6:7).
- Jesus says, *"For where two or three come together in my name, there am I with them"* (Matthew 18:20).

THE LORD NEEDS YOU

The miracle of the loaves and fish is a demonstration and reminder that the Almighty desires to involve you and I in His work. This is why He used a boy's lunch and had the disciples personally distribute the meal.

Certainly, the Creator of all can direct the affairs of this world on His own, but the plan He designed includes the church.

With all power at His disposal, He could *force* man to be subject to His will, yet He has called us to be *"ambassadors"* for Him (2 Corinthians 5:20). The Great Commission is intended to build an army of believers taking the message of Christ to the world.

OFFER WHAT YOU HAVE

Experiencing the miracle first hand, the thousands who were present began to exclaim, *"Surely this is the Prophet who is to come into the world"* (v.14).

Jesus could see that in their exuberance, *"...they intended to come and make him king by force"* (v.15). So He retreated to the mountain to be by Himself.

The Lord's intent was to instill a message of faith in the disciples, however, in the process, many came to know the Messiah.

Friend, offer what you have—large or small—in total trust and belief. You will rejoice at how it will be multiplied.

CHAPTER TEN

THE KEY TO DELIVERANCE

T ension filled the streets of Jerusalem—especially among those who followed Christ.

King Herod decided to reek havoc on many of the church members—and began his campaign of arresting and persecuting believers. *"He had James, the brother of John, put to death with the sword. When he saw that this pleased the Jews, he proceeded to seize Peter also"* (Acts 12:2-3).

All this was happening during the week of the Passover—a perfect time to make a spectacle of the Christians. So Herod had Peter thrown in jail, *"...handing him over to be guarded by four squads of four soldiers, each. Herod intended to bring him out for public trial after the Passover"* (vv.3-4).

However, while Peter was in prison, an army of

believers sprung into action. Scripture records, *"...the church was earnestly praying to God for him"* (v.5).

As the time approached for Peter's release, even though he was under heavy guard, he had no trouble falling asleep between two soldiers—a true demonstration of his peace and stalwart faith.

THIS WAS NO DREAM!

Suddenly, in the middle of the night, an angel appeared by his side and a bright light flooded the cell. The angel shook Peter and told him, *"Quick, get up!"* (v.7).

Then, as the chains fell off his wrists, the angel continued, *"Put on your clothes and sandals...Wrap your cloak around you and follow me"* (v.8).

Peter thought he was dreaming—yet followed the angel's instructions. *"They passed the first and second guards and came to the iron gate leading to the city. It opened for them by itself, and they went through it. When they had walked the length of one street, suddenly the angel left him"* (v.10).

Fully awake, Peter exclaimed, *"Now I know without a doubt that the Lord sent his angel and rescued me from Herod's clutches and from everything the Jewish people were anticipating"* (v.11).

FAITH SETS YOU FREE!

What a simple solution to a colossal problem—just go to sleep and let God take care of the rest!

Why agonize all night long, worrying over a situation which is out of your control? Why lose sleep when it really isn't necessary? Why rehearse imaginary outcomes when God tells you, *"Do not fret because of evil men"* (Proverbs 24:19)? Remember, *"Wait for the Lord, and he will deliver you"* (Proverbs 20:22).

If you have trouble resting at night, turn on a light and begin reading the Word. By filling you mind with God's promises, when you do drift off, your mind will know His perfect peace.

———X———

Faith is the key that opens prison gates and sets you free!

YOUR ROLE IS VITAL

Circumstances may have you caught in a vice-like grip, yet you don't have to remain trapped. In Peter's case, an angel of deliverance appeared, yet it was in response to a disciple who had declared his trust in God.

The reason Peter could lay down his head and fall asleep is because he had placed his entire future in the

Lord's hands.

Please realize that you play a significant part in the eventual outcome of your problem. This is why Jesus said, *"I tell you the truth, if anyone says to this mountain, 'Go, throw yourself into the sea,' and does not doubt in his heart but believes that what he says will happen, it will be done for him"* (Mark 11:23).

This tells us two important things: (1) God has the power to control any situation and (2) we have a crucial role in the process.

It is an example of Xtreme Faith—one who *"does not doubt in his heart."*

COUNT IT AS JOY

Incredible things happen for a man or woman who steps out with boldness and doesn't hesitate. As James tells us, *"...when he asks, he must believe and not doubt, because he who doubts is like a wave of the sea, blown and tossed by the wind. That man should not think he will receive anything from the Lord; he is a double-minded man, unstable in all he does"* (James 1:6-8).

You can't entertain success and defeat at the same time—they are not compatible. This is why Jesus lets us know we must speak in faith and expect what we pray to come to pass.

———————— X ————————

I can tell you from personal experience that without trials you will never know triumph and without heartache you will never know happiness.

A profound statement in God's Word tells us: *"...count it all joy when ye fall into divers temptations"* (James 1:2 KJV).

Why is it joy? The answer is found in the verse 3: *"Knowing this, that the trying of your faith worketh patience."*

AT MIDNIGHT, THEY PRAISED THE LORD

Take a "happiness lesson" from Paul and Silas!

Their preaching at Philippi caused such a commotion, the magistrates ordered them stripped and beaten. *"After they had been severely flogged, they were thrown into prison, and the jailer was commanded to guard them carefully. Upon receiving such orders, he put them in the inner cell and fastened their feet in the stocks"* (Acts 16:23-24).

Instead of having a "Woe is me" pity party, the Bible says, *"About midnight Paul and Silas were praying and singing hymns to God, and the other prisoners were listening to them"* (v.25).

I'm sure these two evangelists were not rejoicing over the pain in their physical bodies—but they were filled with joy knowing their God was able to deliver them from this "gated community."

Without question, their faith was being tested, and in this dark, dank cell, Paul and Silas had every right to complain, yet they stood firm in the belief God knew where they were and had placed a hedge of protection around them.

Suddenly, there was a violent earthquake and the foundations of the prison were shaken. At that moment the prison doors flew open wide and everybody's chains came loose.

"What Must I Do?"

The jailer was jostled from his sleep. When he saw the cell doors open, he drew his sword and was about to commit suicide—because if the prisoners escaped on his watch, he would be as good as dead.

But Paul shouted, *"Don't harm yourself! We are all here!"* (v.28).

Immediately, the keeper of the prison called for lamps to be lit; then he rushed in and fell before Paul and Silas. Trembling, he asked, *"Sirs, what must I do to be saved?"* (v.30).

They replied, *"Believe in the Lord Jesus, and you will be saved—you and your household"* (v.31).

When the jailer led them to his home, Paul and Silas shared their faith and there was great rejoicing because, *"...he had come to believe in God—he and his whole family"* (v.34).

——————— *X* ———————

Today, learn the secret of joy—and you too can sing in every circumstance.

AN UNSEEN HAND

You may not be physically persecuted for your faith as were the early Christians, yet the pressure of this secular world can place you behind its bars. This is why you need more than your human strength and mental resources to survive.

The only way we will ever fulfill the desire God sees for us is to move into the spiritual realm. This is possible when we surrender our will and invite the presence of the Holy Spirit to take control.

Remember, what is natural will eventually fade and die, but what is spiritual lasts forever. As Paul explains, *"...we fix our eyes not on what is seen, but on what is unseen. For what is seen is temporary, but what is unseen is eternal"* (2 Corinthians 4:18).

————————✗————————

Rejoice! You don't need to remain confined to life's prison. The unseen hand of God will liberate and set you free!

A DRAMATIC MESSAGE

One of the least-known religious figures in the New Testament is a prophet from Jerusalem named Agabus.

Following one of Paul's missionary journeys, he returned to Caesarea, staying at the home of Philip, the evangelist.

Agabus came down to meet him—and the encounter proved to be quite dramatic. He marched up to Paul, removed his belt and tied himself up. Of course, there was a meaning behind this demonstration.

The prophet told Paul, *"The Holy Spirit says, 'In this way the Jews of Jerusalem will bind the owner of this belt and will hand him over to the Gentiles'"* (Acts 21:11).

The people who heard these words begged Paul to change his travel plans and avoid going to Jerusalem, but he refused. Paul said, *"Why are you weeping and breaking my heart? I am ready not only to be bound, but also to die in Jerusalem for the name of the Lord Jesus"* (13).

Knowing Agabus' prophecy was true, Paul still felt this is exactly what God wanted to happen—and besides, it would be a great opportunity to tell the Roman officials about Jesus.

Xtreme Faith doesn't see obstacles, only opportunities. After all the apostle had endured, what was one more confrontation on the road to fulfilling the Great Commission?

AN ANGRY MOB

Upon arriving in Jerusalem, the prophet's warning proved to be accurate. When those who hated the Christians spotted Paul at the temple, they incited a riot against him and soon, *"The whole city was aroused, and the people came running from all directions. Seizing Paul, they dragged him from the temple"* (v.30).

Immediately, Roman soldiers rushed over to arrest Paul and threw him in prison. They were protecting him from the wrath of the angry mob and holding him until the authorities could determine if he had, indeed, committed any offenses.

Paul persuaded the warden to allow him to speak to the upset crowd, and he shared his personal testimony of how he, as Saul, once persecuted Christians, but had a

Damascus Road experience which transformed his life.

Still, the critics would not be appeased. They shouted, *"Rid the earth of him! He's not fit to live!"* (Acts 22:22).

Concerned for his safety, the soldiers had Paul moved to another prison, where he had the opportunity to plead his case before King Agrippa, whom the Romans had placed as ruler over Judah.

A Blessing in Disguise

Paul's articulate defense before the King was without parallel. In the palace court, the missionary-evangelist proclaimed, *"I was not disobedient to the vision from heaven. First to those in Damascus, then to those in Jerusalem and in all Judea, and to the Gentiles also, I preached that they should repent and turn to God and prove their repentance by their deeds. That is why the Jews seized me in the temple courts and tried to kill me. But I have had God's help to this very day, and so I stand here and testify to small and great alike. I am saying nothing beyond what the prophets and Moses said would happen—that the Christ would suffer and, as the first to rise from the dead, would proclaim light to his own people and to the Gentiles"* (Acts 26:19-23).

After his strong defense—which was truly a profound Gospel message, King Agrippa responded to Paul, *"Almost thou persuadest me to be a Christian"* (v.28).

The punishment handed down to the apostle Paul was a blessing in disguise. He was sent to Rome: *"Boldly and without hindrance he preached the kingdom of God and taught about the Lord Jesus Christ"* (Acts 28:31).

The lesson learned by Peter, Paul and Silas still rings true today. Faith is the key to your deliverance!

CHAPTER ELEVEN

A New Declaration

The process of developing Xtreme faith includes having a lifestyle that is based on God's Word. The Lord doesn't expect you to live a dull, monotonous, unfulfilled existence.

Long ago King Solomon wrote, *"...I realized that it is good and proper for a man to eat and drink, and to find satisfaction in his toilsome labor under the sun during the few days of life God has given him—for this is his lot"* (Ecclesiastes 5:18).

He continued, *" Moreover, when God gives any man wealth and possessions, and enables him to enjoy them, to accept his lot and be happy in his work—this is a gift of God. He seldom reflects on the days of his life, because God keeps him occupied with gladness of heart"* (Ecclesiastes 5:19-20).

It is time to discard the image of yourself as a lonely pilgrim traveling down a road filled with potholes of worry, doubt, poverty and fear.

God declares you are an overcomer *now*—not someday on the other side of the Jordan: *"...for everyone born of God overcomes the world. This is the victory that has overcome the world, even our faith"* (1 John 5:4).

Remember, you have been made "right" through the Savior (2 Corinthians 5:21) and *"This righteousness from God comes through faith in Jesus Christ to all who believe"* (Romans 3:22).

As a result, Satan no longer exerts dominion over you because the one who is *"...born of God* [is] *safe, and the evil one cannot harm him"* (1 John 5:18).

———— *X* ————

Satan can try every angle of deception, but you will triumph because in God's Son, you are victorious.

FROM TEARS TO A TESTIMONY

Every time you declare who you are in Christ, your inner man—spirit and soul—is strengthened. As the process continues, you become a confident, self-assured Christian who walks as a child of the King and speaks with authority.

"Overcoming" has nothing to do with human persuasion or pressure. It is the natural by-product of living with the principles and promises of God.

We should take a lesson from David. At one point he cried, *"I am worn out from groaning; all night long I flood my bed with weeping and drench my couch with tears. My eyes grow weak with sorrow; they fail because of all my foes"* (Psalm 6:6-7).

How was he able to escape this trap of self-defeat? David writes, *"I waited patiently for the Lord; he turned to me and heard my cry. He lifted me out of the slimy pit, out of the mud and mire; he set my feet on a rock and gave me a firm place to stand"* (Psalm 40:1-2).

As a result, he was soon able to declare with confidence, *"Let God arise, let his enemies be scattered"* (Psalm 68:1 KJV).

Because he had walked through the dark valleys and discovered the answers, there came a day when he could counsel others. In Psalm 91 David is not referring to his personal troubles; he is testifying—sharing the keys to victory with someone else: *"Surely he will save you from the fowler's snare and from the deadly pestilence. He will cover you with his feathers, and under his wings you will find refuge; his faithfulness will be your shield and rampart. You will not fear the terror of night, nor the*

133

arrow that flies by day, nor the pestilence that stalks in the darkness, nor the plague that destroys at midday. A thousand may fall at your side, ten thousand at your right hand, but it will not come near you" (Psalm 91:3-7).

David came a long way from crying himself to sleep!

"Shame on You"

My heart goes out to children who are raised in homes where they are told daily—in hundreds of ways:

- "Don't be so stupid."
- "You'll never amount to anything."
- "Who could love somebody like you?"
- "You will never make a name for yourself."
- "You're the laziest kid I've ever seen."
- "Why can't you finish what you start?"
- "You'll never be college material"
- "Shame on you!"

Over time, being labeled as inferior becomes so etched in the children's subconsciousness, they eventually begins to act out this self-fulfilling prophecy.

This distorted image not only results in a rejection of personal potential, but can block out the vision God has planned for their future.

RAIN IS ON THE WAY!

The individual who is addicted to cigarettes or alcohol has probably said a thousand times, "I can't quit." However, those very words reinforce the habit, sowing negative seeds which are as harmful as the nicotine or drug itself. And the more that phrase is repeated, the stronger the hold of the addiction becomes.

———X———

If the Bible proclaims "You can do all things," start believing and confessing, "I can stop smoking," or "I can stop drinking."

The same principle applies to living in poverty. There are millions of third and fourth generation families who cannot break free from the spirit or mentality of living in lack. They see no way out—which means they are likely to remain in the same financial situation for a lifetime.

However, God's Word declares He will *"...send you rain for the seed you sow in the ground, and the food that comes from the land will be rich and plentiful"* (Isaiah 30:23).

Stand on this declaration: *"The house of the righteous contains great treasure"* (Proverbs 15:6).

As a child of the King, everything in heaven and earth belongs to you.

Health is Yours

To many, sickness becomes habit-forming.

I'm sure you've met them—people who have a slight fever and think it's a serious virus, or sneeze once and worry, "I must be coming down with the flu."

————— X —————

If certain individuals didn't have a litany of medical problems, they wouldn't have anything to talk about!

This is not how God intends for His children to live. He sends His Word to bring you health and healing (Psalm 107:20) and wants to provide *"...health to your body and nourishment to your bones"* (Proverbs 3:8).

Both your spiritual and physical well being were bought with the blood of Christ at Calvary. As the psalmist proclaimed—even before it happened—*"Praise the Lord, O my soul, and forget not all his benefits—who forgives all your sins and heals all your diseases"* (Psalm 103:2-3).

Stand on your faith and declare what Christ has

provided for you.

HOPE FOR TOMORROW

If you dwell on misfortune, it will surely head your way—and when your mind is filled with negative scenarios, you are opening the wrong doors.

Job reached the point where he realized, *"What I feared has come upon me; what I dreaded has happened to me"* (Job 3:25).

Those who keep thinking of calamity become like the people described by David: *"There they were, overwhelmed with dread, where there was nothing to dread"* (Psalm 53:5).

My friend, God can help you erase both the fear of the future and the memory of a negative past. His objective is to give you hope for the future: *"For God hath not given us the spirit of fear; but of power, and of love, and of a sound mind"* (2 Timothy 1:7 KJV).

If the Lord can bury your yesterday and never remember it against you, why can't you do the same?

A NEW ATTITUDE

In God's sight we are all born equal—neither superior or inferior: We have each been given a *"measure of faith"* on which to build our lives (Romans 12:3).

As we grow and develop, there are certainly areas where we need God's help for improvement, yet we should never hesitate to celebrate the gifts and talents we already posesses.

Whether your attitudes are the result of culture, environment or your own carnality, with God's help, you can reclaim your life and eliminate what is not pleasing in His sight. For example the Bible tells you to, *"...rid yourselves of...anger, rage, malice, slander, and filthy language from your lips...since you have taken off your old self with its practices and have put on the new self, which is being renewed in knowledge in the image of its Creator"* (Colossians 3:8-10).

Through a personal relationship with Christ:

- You can have new thoughts (Romans 12:2).
- You can experience a new attitude (Ephesians 4:23).
- You can enjoy a new life (Romans 6:4).

Jesus died on the cross, *"...so that his life may be revealed in our mortal body"* (2 Corinthians 4:11). We are being transformed from what we were into what He is. Praise His Name!

HIS TREASURE

If you want to know how much you are worth, think

for a moment that God sent His only Son to earth to die for you. Visualize Him with His arms outstretched on a cruel cross, saying, "I love you *this* much."

─────────X─────────

The Creator not only made you,
He values your life.

You were *"fearfully and wonderfully made"* (Psalm 139:14), *"And he will never forsake his inheritance"* (Psalm 94:14).

Jesus says, *"Look at the birds of the air; they do not sow or reap or store away in barns, and yet your heavenly Father feeds them. Are you not much more valuable than they?"* (Matthew 6:26).

It's true: you are the Lord's treasure.

SEEK HIS WILL

If you know Christ as your Savior, you are an heir to the promise made to Abraham—and have access to the resources of heaven.

Scripture tells us, *"...those who have faith are blessed along with Abraham, the man of faith...[God] redeemed us in order that the blessing given to Abraham might come to the Gentiles through Christ Jesus, so that by faith we might receive the promise of the Spirit"* (Galatians 3:9,14).

The question is often asked, "If we are to receive the promises of Abraham, why do so few believers walk in them?"

There are several reasons, including traditions, negative attitudes and an unwillingness to accept what the Bible teaches regarding God's favor and blessing.

One of the greatest mistakes believers make is to seek their personal desires before determining what the Lord has planned for them. They quote, "Whatever I ask I will receive," yet that is not what Scripture teaches.

Read this verse carefully: *"This is the confidence we have in approaching God: that if we ask anything according to his will, he hears us"* (1 John 5:14).

Whose will? His!

When you are linked with the Father's desires and wishes, He will *"...do exceeding abundantly above all that we ask or think"* (Ephesians 3:20 KJV).

DESTROY FAILURE

Who are you going to believe, God Almighty or your own carnal mind? Scripture is describing you when it says, *"He is like a tree planted by streams of water, which yields its fruit in season and whose leaf does not wither. Whatever he does prospers"* (Psalm 1:3).

If this is true, why should you continue speaking failure? Make a decision to *"...demolish arguments and every pretension that sets itself up against the knowledge of God"* (2 Corinthians 10:5).

- When your mind says, "I don't know which way to turn," God declares, *"I will instruct you and teach you in the way you should go; I will counsel you and watch over you"* (Psalm 32:8).
- When your body says, "I am under too much stress," the Lord promises, *"Peace I leave with you; my peace I give you...Do not let your hearts be troubled and do not be afraid"* (John 14:27).
- When your heart says, "I am fearful of tomorrow," declare, *"The Lord is my light and my salvation—whom shall I fear?"* (Psalm 27:1).

"I AM STRONG"

Critics love to argue, "Why should you affirm something which is contrary to reality. Isn't that dishonest?"

No, speaking in faith is a spiritual principle God endorses. There was nothing but darkness when the

Creator said, *"Let there be light"* (Genesis 1:3). This is why the Lord tells you and me, *"...let the weak say, I am strong"* (Joel 3:10 KJV).

———— X ————

God sees the manifestation before it exists and what He says will become reality.

On the authority of Jesus, *"I tell you the truth, until heaven and earth disappear, not the smallest letter, not the least stroke of a pen, will by any means disappear from the Law until everything is accomplished"* (Matthew 5:18). When you declare what the Lord has promised, you are standing on solid ground.

A SELF-INVENTORY

Please take the time to carefully examine your vision and your vocabulary.

If you are picturing a future which is depressing and bleak, God can place a dream within you as powerful as the one He gave to Joseph. When the Lord's vision becomes the driving force, it doesn't matter how others treat you. Even if they meant to bring you harm, you can say, *"...God intended it for good"* (Genesis 50:20).

Take a self-inventory of your words. Do they speak

of faith, belief and expectation?

Since the Lord is waiting to pour out blessings beyond measure, we must not interfere with His plans by speaking words of gloom and despair.

You are chosen by God to be part of His royal family. I pray you will *"...declare the praises of him who called you out of darkness into his wonderful light"* (1 Peter 2:9).

Make a new declaration today!

CHAPTER TWELVE

"ACCORDING TO YOUR FAITH"

I was recently asked, "Pastor Thomas, why is it so easy for you to pray for miracles?"

Thinking about the question for a moment, I responded, "When you've seen a miracle first-hand, your doubts are settled. You believe God can heal anyone, anytime, anywhere."

In fact, the first healing you witness becomes a life changing experience—not just for the person who has received a touch from God, but for *you!* It confirms and expands your faith, becoming a launching pad which multiplies your ministry in ways you can never imagine.

A TIME OF TESTING

I can vividly remember the days when, fresh out of

Bible College, I became the youth pastor at a thriving church in Fort Lauderdale, Florida, pastored by George Miller—who has since gone on to be with the Lord.

This precious man of God had a tremendous healing ministry and I stood beside him week after week as he prayed the prayer of faith for people who were suffering with all kinds of infirmities. The testimonies of healing were incredible.

My belief was encouraged, Pastor Miller was praying for the needs, and I was his assistant. However, I had never been put in a place where my personal faith had to be tested.

COVERED IN SORES

Then one Sunday morning, I was with the pastor and we were laying hands on those who had come forward for healing. It was a time of great rejoicing.

As we were moving along the "prayer line" which had formed, I noticed a tall, thin man, at least six-feet-four with blond-gray hair. He was towering over us.

I vaguely recognized him, since he and his wife had been attending the church for a short time.

As Pastor Miller was busy praying with an individual, the man motioned for me to come over to him. As I did, I looked up and could see his face was literally covered with skin cancer. He had ugly sores all over his face and

I had never seen a condition so severe.

Immediately I thought, "This man really needs Pastor Miller to pray for him."

Almost as quickly as this entered my mind, the gentleman looked at me and shared, "God just spoke to me and said you are to pray for me—and I will be healed."

"NO, NO," THE MAN INSISTED

Wow! I could almost feel the blood drain from my body and suddenly I felt woozy. I was thinking, "Lord, I have never *personally* seen anyone healed as the result of my prayers, only when there is someone believing with me." So, I told him, "Pastor Miller will be here in just a moment and we are going to be in agreement together."

"No, no," he insisted. "You are the one who is supposed to lay hands on me and pray in order for me to receive my healing."

———— *X* ————

Quickly, I prayed, "God, I need you to increase my faith."

I never doubted the Lord *could* heal, but would God

use me as a vehicle by which the miracle would take place?

"Are you sure you heard from God?" I asked him.

"Absolutely," he replied.

"Okay, sir," I told him. "I know we serve a healing God, and I'm going to believe the Lord with you for a complete miracle."

Then I reached up as high as my arms could and placed my hand on his forehead—and when I felt the sores on his face, my faith was severely tested. Echoing in my spirit was what the man had previously told me: "If you pray for me, I will be healed."

I began fervently calling on God. "Father, in the name of Jesus, let healing virtue flow through this person. Cause this skin cancer to wither and die. Let it leave his body and never return again. Father, I decree total healing and complete restoration."

I COULDN'T LOOK

I was such a young, novice minister, I'm sure some of my words were just repeating what I heard the pastor say. But in my heart, I was believing for a miracle.

As I finished praying, I remember bringing my hand down and I didn't even look at him. I turned away because I did not want anything to weaken the faith I felt as I prayed.

As the service progressed, I continued to earnestly pray for a miracle for this dear man. Inwardly, I knew the Lord had healed him, yet I felt I could not look in his direction.

———————— X ————————

Some may say, "What weak faith,"
yet I didn't want to give the enemy a
possible foothold to challenge me.

"WHAT HAPPENED?"

The next morning, at about 11 o'clock, I received a call from the gentleman. "Do you mind if I come by to see you and Pastor Miller?"

"That will be fine," I responded. "Come right over."

When he arrived both of us were waiting, and the moment he walked in the office we hardly recognized him. Yes, this was the same tall man, but his skin was as smooth and healthy as a newborn baby's face. The sores were totally gone! We looked at him and asked, "What happened?"

He turned to me and exclaimed, "When you prayed for me there was a sensation that washed all over my body—like a burning. It stayed on me all afternoon and all night."

Then, smiling from ear to ear, he continued, "When I got up this morning and I took my shower, all of those ugly scabs and sores washed off my face, my arms and my body. Look at me! I'm totally and completely healed. You can't even tell that I ever had a problem. You prayed total restoration and I have no scars, Pastor!"

From that day forward, I have never had the slightest hesitation praying for any need.

————— *X* —————

There is nothing too big or small for the Almighty to perform. He is still a prayer-answering God.

Xtreme Faith begins to make itself known when you realize it's not *your* human ability, rather the God you serve who brings results.

WHO SHOULD CALL?

One of the most misunderstood passages of Scripture deals with healing. James writes, *"Is any sick among you? Let him call for the elders of the church; and let them pray over him, anointing him with oil in the name of the Lord: And the prayer of faith shall save the sick, and the Lord shall raise him up"* (James 5:14 KJV).

Examine those words closely. James is saying, "If

there are people around you who are sick, they (the infirmed, not the elders) should call the elders to pray." Faith for healing should begin with the person needing a miracle—just as the man with the skin cancer asked me to pray for him.

Why should the sick call for the elders? Because those who are weak in faith need help moving beyond their present circumstances.

You see, healing is already theirs; they only need to reach out and claim it. Christ did the work on Calvary: *"Who his own self bare our sins in his own body on the tree, that we, being dead to sins, should live unto righteousness: by whose stripes ye were healed"* (1 Peter 2:24 KJV).

The Word doesn't say, "you can be healed," "you may by healed" or "you will be healed." No, "you *were* healed." It is a finished work of the cross.

In the words of the prophet Isaiah, *"But he was wounded for our transgressions, he was bruised for our iniquities: the chastisement of our peace was upon him; and with his stripes we are healed"* (Isaiah 53:5 KJV).

Hallelujah! You *were* healed—and you *are* healed!

FAITH IS RELEASED

When those in ministry anoint the sick with oil and pray for healing, they are giving a visual reminder of what was purchased for us over 2000 years ago on Golgotha.

When the physical presence of a representative of the Lord (an elder or minister) joins forces with the symbolic presence of the Holy Spirit (the oil), faith is released and a miracle-working God provides what Jesus has already accomplished.

Thank the Lord for those who help us reach beyond our faith and take hold of God's provision.

OUR CREATIVE LORD

Some believers try to confine the Lord to a box and say, "There is only one way you can receive your healing—and here is exactly what you must do."

Eventually they will learn we serve a creative Lord who touches our lives in myriad ways:

- Jesus spoke the Word and the servant of the Roman centurion was healed (Matthew 8).
- He touched the hand of Peter's mother-in-law and her fever left (Matthew 8).
- He anointed the eyes of a blind man with spittle and clay, and his sight was restored (John 9).
- He cleansed the ten lepers *"as they went"* (Luke 17).

However, there is one common denominator occurring in all of these miracles—faith. To the woman who touched His garment, Jesus said *"...thy faith hath made thee whole"* (Matthew 9:22 KJV).

There are even times when the Lord brings the answer, not as the result of your belief, but through the strong faith of others.

THROUGH THE ROOF!

In the early days of Jesus' ministry, just a mention that the "Miracle Worker" was nearby produced large crowds.

Once, in Capernaum, where He was ministering at a home, the crowd which gathered was so large no one could come in or out of the entrance.

Four men carried a paraplegic to Him on a stretcher. And when they couldn't get in, they climbed up on the roof, removed part of the structure, and lowered the bed down to Jesus.

As Scripture records the event, *"When Jesus saw their faith..."* (Mark 2:5). Whose faith? It wasn't that of the paraplegic; it was the faith of the four men.

The Lord told the deformed man, *"...take your mat and go home"* (v.11).

In full view of everyone present, the man carried his bed and walked out of the house. *"This amazed everyone and they praised God, saying, 'We have never seen anything like this!'"* (v.12).

God honors *all* faith—regardless of its source.

HE SEES YOUR HEART

The disciples and followers of Christ who continued His miracle ministry, inspired faith in many ways. People were healed in Peter's shadow, and pieces of cloth which had been worn by Paul brought healing and deliverance.

Whether you lift your hands high or cup them in worship is not as important as what the Lord sees in your heart. I have witnessed people healed who were standing, sitting, kneeling, even stretched out on a hospital bed!

Some loudly rebuke sickness, others quote healing verses, and still others quietly wait before the throne of grace. Yet, each receives according to his or her faith.

Remember, *"There are differences of administrations, but the same Lord. And there are diversities of operations, but it is the same God which worketh all in all"* (1 Corinthians 12:5-6 KJV).

Healing is not the result of the process, rather in the stripes Jesus suffered on the cross.

DECLARE THE ANSWER

Xtreme Faith must never be concerned with techniques or procedures; it must be about the source of your hope, expectation and belief.

In a time when there is much written on the topic of "positive confession," I've been asked, "What about the man who says, 'I am not sick,' when his face is drawn and ashen white, and he can't stop coughing?"

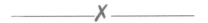

I believe in doctors and those in the medical profession, but I also know that our entire immune system reacts to the information we feed it.

I would much rather claim God's promises for healing than to continually tell myself, "I feel bad and I think I'm getting worse."

Never be ashamed to declare that the healing Christ purchased for you on the cross is truly yours—even if you can't see its immediate manifestation in your body. Stand on the Word and claim you are a partaker of His divine nature (2 Peter 1:4) and are going *"from glory to glory"* (2 Corinthians 3:18).

MORE THAN ENOUGH

Starting this very moment, the Lord wants you to stretch your faith from minus to plus, from want to wondrous, from insufficiency to abundance.

Saturate yourself with promises and possibilities found in God's Word. While certain speakers and books may motivate you, there is no substitute for receiving directly from the Father.

Begin hearing with spiritual ears, knowing that before we experience favor on earth, the work takes place above. God has *"...blessed us in the heavenly realms with every spiritual blessing in Christ"* (Ephesians 1:3).

Next, tap into the Father's storehouse: *"His divine power has given us everything we need for life and godliness through our knowledge of him who called us by his own glory and goodness"* (2 Peter 1:3).

Then, since *more* than enough is available, take the lid off your thinking! *"Now to him who is able to do immeasurably more than all we ask or imagine, according to his power that is at work within us"* (Ephesians 3:20).

Finally, let the Lord bless the purpose and task to which He has called you. *"And God is able to make all grace abound to you, so that in all things at all times, having all that you need, you will abound in every good work"* (2 Corinthians 9:8).

EXPERIENCE THE EVIDENCE

The principles of faith I have shared in these pages, are more than ideas and concepts. They are God's plan for your daily living—and He expects you to put them into practice.

Remember:

- Ultimate faith was established from the foundation of the world (Revelation 13:8).
- Expectation cannot be self-produced; it must come from above (Psalm 62:5).
- You can know the mind of the Lord (Philippians 2:5).
- Faith is a gift from God (Ephesians 2:8).
- Your Heavenly Father promises to supply all your needs (Philippians. 4:19).
- Obedience is required for abundance (Isaiah 1:19).
- Your faith is expanded when you join with others in agreement (Matthew 18:19).
- God gives you a pattern for success (Hebrews 8:5).
- Nothing is too difficult for the Lord (Genesis 18:14).

I believe the gift God has placed within you will

multiply beyond measure—and you will see the evidence in your family, career, health and spiritual life.

May you personally experience the continual favor and eternal blessings of Xtreme Faith.

FOR A COMPLETE LIST OF MINISTRY TOOLS BY
DR. RICK THOMAS,
CONTACT:

SEED OF HARVEST MINISTRIES
1490 Banks Road
Margate, Florida 33063
954-973-0152
www.seedofharvest.org